WHY IS GOD LAUGHING?

DeePAK CHOPRA

WHY IS GOD LAUGHING?

One Man's Journey to Joy and Spiritual Optimism

RIDER

LONDON · SYDNEY · AUCKLAND · JOHANNESBURG

1 3 5 7 9 10 8 6 4 2

Published in 2008 by Rider, an imprint of Ebury Publishing
First published in the USA by Harmony Books, an imprint of the Crown
Publishing Group, a division of Random House, Inc., New York, in 2008

Ebury Publishing is a Random House Group company

The Random House Group Limited Reg. No. 954009

Addresses for companies within the Random House Group can be found at
www.rbooks.co.uk

A CIP catalogue record for this book is available from the British Library

The Random House Group Limited supports The Forest Stewardship
Council (FSC), the leading international forest certification organisation.
All our titles that are printed on Greenpeace approved FSC certified paper
carry the FSC logo. Our paper procurement policy can be found at
www.rbooks.co.uk/environment

Mixed Sources
Product group from well-managed
forests and other controlled sources
www.fsc.org Cert no. TT-COC-2139
© 1996 Forest Stewardship Council

Printed and bound in Great Britain by Clays of St Ives PLC

ISBN 9781846041402 (hardback)
ISBN 9781846041419 (paperback)

Copies are available at special rates for bulk orders. Contact the sales
development team on 020 7840 8487 for more information.

To buy books by your favourite authors and register for offers, visit www.rbooks.co.uk

To Mike Myers,

who showed me that true spirituality means

not taking ourselves too seriously, and to lovers of

laughter and wisdom everywhere

CONTENTS

Photo by Mark Seliger

FOREWORD

I'VE HAD MANY HEROES IN MY LIFE. MY FATHER WAS the first; Deepak Chopra the most recent. There was one hero in between who taught me about laughter. His name was Del Close.

Del Close was one of the founders of the Second City Theatre in Chicago in 1959. He is the father of modern improvised comedy as we know it, a leader of the American satire boom, the inventor of the "happening," a philosopher, a theorist, a great teacher, and most important he was funny—and he knew funny. Bill Murray, John Belushi, Chris Farley, Stephen Colbert, Amy Poehler, myself, and many others have all benefited from his teaching and his philosophy that comedy equals truth and truth equals spiritual growth. Plainly put, "ha-ha" is related to "ah-ha," the sound one makes upon the realization of truth.

They say that the truth may set you free, but I find that the truth can be very painful at first. As Lenny Bruce once said, the equation for comedy is "laughter = pain +

time." Del would call the plus time "distance"; Deepak would call it "detachment." Both would agree that to be enlightened you must travel lightly.

Laughing feels good. In a fast-paced and entertaining form, *Why Is God Laughing?* lays out the spiritual/healthful nature of laughter as well as the mindset of detachment, gratitude, and brave truth-seeking that fosters such laughter and the inner peace that results.

My first hero, my father, used to say, "Nothing's so bad that it can't be laughed at." An intense man, he still found humor in the darkest moments. My father lived through the Depression, the "Phony War" in 1939, World War II, the Cold War, and ultimately his own war with Alzheimer's. But even in his dementia he could find humor in his own condition: so strong and innately human is the need to laugh.

Henri Bergson, in his essay *Laughter,* said that laughter is an autonomic response from deep in the reptilian part of our brain, and that it is triggered by the realization of our own mortality. In these pages Deepak has managed to dramatize this brilliantly in the form of Mickey Fellows, a comedian forced to face his darkest fears. Deepak shows us that there is darkness in the world and that comedy is a candle; he encourages us to meditate on the candle and not the darkness.

Why is God laughing? He gets the joke.

—MIKE MYERS

WHY IS GOD LAUGHING?

1

GRACE SHINES LIKE A SLIVER OF LIGHT. IT PENE-trates the universe, undeterred by distance or darkness. You won't see it, but it knows where it is going. At any moment someone may be touched by its mysterious power.

Even Mickey Fellows.

On this particular day Mickey was speeding through the Valley in his black Cadillac Escalade, keeping half an eye out for police. The L.A. sun glared off the freeway, but for Mickey, sitting behind his tinted windows and wraparound shades, it could have been twilight.

"Say that again," he muttered into his cell phone.

"The club owners aren't happy. They say the new material isn't funny. They want the old Mickey back." It was Alicia, his agent.

"Screw 'em. They should kiss my derriere that I even bother to show up."

Mickey Fellows had movie offers from two studios. His last divorce had made the cover of *People* magazine.

The only reason he worked the comedy clubs at all was to keep his feel for the audience.

Alicia didn't back down. "You don't want to play it that way. You may need those clubs some day."

"God forbid." Mickey lit up another menthol Merit.

God has the advantage of witnessing every lifetime at once, erasing all differences. If you could look down on the human race from an infinite distance, you'd see Everyman was on the freeway that day. Like the rest of us, Mickey gave little thought to his soul. He didn't want to face painful truths, so he managed to distract himself almost every waking hour.

At this moment, Mickey figured it was time for a laugh. "I've got a good one for you," he told his agent. "My grandfather's eighty years old, and he still has sex almost every day. He almost had it on Monday, he almost had it on Tuesday, he almost had it on Wednesday."

Alicia was silent.

"I think I have another call coming in," said Mickey.

"No, you don't."

"I'm not kidding this time," Mickey said. "Hold on." He pushed a button. "Hello?"

"Is this Michael Fellows?"

"Who wants to know?" Strangers were always getting his number.

"I'm calling from Cedars-Sinai Hospital."

Mickey felt a bead of sweat roll down his neck. He gripped the wheel tighter. "Yes?"

In the few seconds between an impending disaster and its crash to earth, an amazing number of thoughts can race through your mind. Mickey saw himself at his annual physical the week before. His wife's face flashed before him, as clearly as if they hadn't been divorced for five years. Cancer, AIDS, car accident. Fate's wheel was spinning, and the arrow was about to stop.

"I'm sorry, Mr. Fellows. It's your father."

"Did he fall? Someone's supposed to be watching him," Mickey said. He had hired a full-time housekeeper for his father, a placid Guatemalan lady who knew little English.

"Your father got the best care in the ER. Everything possible was done to revive him, but he couldn't be saved."

Mickey didn't hear those last words. As soon as the voice said "everything possible was done," a roar in Mickey's ears drowned out everything else.

"When did he die?"

The voice on the phone, a woman's and probably a nurse, started to explain, but the roar kept blocking it out.

"Wait a second," said Mickey, pulling off onto the shoulder of the road. He breathed deeply, and shook his head, like a swimmer knocking water out of his ears. "Could you repeat that?"

"He was brought in unconscious by EMS. It was a massive coronary. Your name was in his wallet as next of kin."

Mickey felt faintly nauseous. "Did he suffer?"

The voice tried to sound reassuring. "If it's any comfort, this kind of heart attack is usually quick, less than a minute."

A minute that felt like hours, Mickey thought. "All right, I'll be right there. Will I find him in the ER?"

The woman's voice said yes, and Mickey hung up. He pulled back out into traffic and raced to the next exit. The news had come as a shock, but he didn't cry. He didn't know how to feel, really. Larry. The old man. Mickey's mother had died young, of breast cancer. Her side of the family was prone to it. His father on the other hand was tough as nails. A joke popped uninvited into Mickey's head.

A middle-aged woman drops dead of a heart attack. When she gets to Heaven, God says, "There's been a terrible mistake. You're not due to die for another forty years."

The woman wakes up and goes home. She figures she's got

such a long life ahead of her, she might as well look good. So she goes in for plastic surgery—face-lift, boob job, tummy tuck, the works. Two months later she's crossing the street and a bus hits her.

This time when she gets to Heaven, she says to God, "What's going on? I was supposed to live another forty years."

And God says, "Mabel, is that you?"

Usually Mickey found comfort in his own jokes, but this one was followed by a wave of guilt. It was no time for humor, yet that was how his mind worked. He couldn't help it.

The ER waiting room was a tense place, the air heavy with suffering. Desperate faces glanced up at anyone passing by, hoping it might be a doctor. Mickey marched up to the admitting desk. When the nurse heard his name, she said, "I'm sorry for your loss, Mr. Fellows. This way, please."

She led him through a set of swinging doors and down a corridor lined with gurneys. On one of them a boy with his head swathed in bloody bandages sat upright, softly moaning. They stopped at the swinging doors at the end of the hall, and the nurse stood aside.

"Are you ready?" she asked.

"Give me a moment, will you?" said Mickey.

"Take your time. The doctor will be right inside whenever you're ready," she murmured.

To settle his nerves, Mickey tried to imagine how Larry's face would look in death. Instead, another joke popped into his head.

God and the Devil were arguing about the fence that separates Heaven and Hell. "Your side's falling down," said God. "Just look at it."

"So what?" said the Devil.

"We're both responsible for keeping up our side. Mine is perfect."

The Devil shrugged indifferently. "So what are you going to do about it?"

"If you force me to, I'll get a lawyer and sue you," said God.

The Devil only laughed. "Give me a break. Where are you gonna find a lawyer?"

Mickey chuckled, then he caught himself. "Jesus, why can't I act normal?" he muttered.

"Pardon me?" said the nurse.

"Nothing. I'll go in now. Thank you."

Somehow, in his entire thirty-seven years, Mickey had never seen a corpse. The lights in the room had been dimmed. A shape lay under a sheet on a table.

Jesus, Dad. You couldn't give me a heads up?

It was amazing how death stilled the air around it.

Mickey pondered that and tried not to shiver. The smell of disinfectant made the room feel colder than it was. Minutes passed. Mickey pinched himself, trying not to think of another joke.

A Catholic, a Protestant, and a Jew die and go to Heaven. At the pearly gates St. Peter says—

Somebody coughed softly next to him. "Mr. Fellows? I'm Dr. Singh."

The joke flew out of Mickey's mind. He turned to the Indian man in green hospital garb with a stethoscope around his neck.

"I didn't mean to intrude," the young doctor murmured. He looked like he could be twenty, except for his bristly black beard.

Mickey felt a twinge of guilt. *He thinks I was praying.*

The doctor made a reassuring motion with his hand. "You can come closer, if you want," he said. Neither of them spoke as the young doctor pulled the sheet back.

It wasn't nearly as hard to look as Mickey had feared. His father could have been sleeping. Larry's color wasn't pale yet. Even at seventy he was a demon for keeping a good suntan all year.

"He looks peaceful."

Dr. Singh nodded. "Do you want to know exactly what happened? I wasn't on duty when he came in, but

I've reviewed his chart. Sometimes family members want details."

"Just a few," Mickey said. He wondered if most sons would be reaching under the sheet to grab their father's hand. Larry's hands were folded over his chest. Would it be creepier if the flesh felt warm or cold?

"It was an acute myocardial infarction. A massive heart attack, at around two this afternoon. Paramedics showed up inside of five minutes. But your father was probably dead before he hit the floor."

Mickey said, "So it was quick."

"Very."

Maybe that accounted for the expression on Larry's face, which wasn't really peaceful, Mickey observed, but slightly surprised. If your heart was exploding and all you felt was excruciating pain, would you just look surprised? Suddenly Mickey had a new idea that caught him off guard.

I'm not dead, you chump. I'm just fooling, and I went to a lot of trouble here. You get the joke, don't you? You, of all people.

Mickey had to fight his sudden impulse to kick over the table and knock his old man onto the floor.

That's not funny, you sick bastard, he'd shout. And Larry would explode into one of his big belly laughs as he got up and dusted himself off.

Then Mickey caught the doctor's expression out of the corner of his eye. Was that nervousness Mickey saw? The young doctor might be green—maybe he hadn't seen that much death himself. Mickey couldn't tell. But one thing he knew for sure. The situation definitely wasn't a joke.

THREE DAYS LATER Mickey went to close up his father's apartment. It was a small one-bedroom, part of a retirement complex in Culver City. He paid off Lupe, the Guatemalan housekeeper. She was the one who had found Larry's body.

"There, señor," she said, pointing to Larry's favorite chair, a Barcalounger that Mickey remembered from when he was a boy. It had been through the wars, the dark blue leather arms worn and cracked

So that's where you bought it, Mickey thought.

After Lupe left, giggling with embarrassment—he had slipped her an extra hundred and hauled her battered vacuum cleaner out to her car—there was no reason to stick around. Mickey pulled the blinds, shutting out the last feeble rays of twilight. He turned the thermostat down and looked around.

Anything else?

He found a half-empty whiskey bottle on his father's bedside table. The label read "Jim Beam," but screamed loneliness. Mickey wondered if his father had completely given up toward the end. He had always sounded upbeat on the phone.

"Naw, you don't have to run over here. Your old man's fit as a fiddle and tight as a drum," Larry would say. "Or maybe just tight."

Mickey swirled the amber liquor around absent-mindedly. Tight was right.

When he drifted through the shadowy living room, bottle in hand, Mickey plopped down in the beat-up lounger, unscrewed the top, and took a long swig. He held the bottle up, imagining a toast to the departed.

> *Here's to Sally, who dresses in black,*
> *She always looks hot, she never looks back.*
> *And when Sally kisses, she kisses so sweet,*
> *She makes a thing stand that never had feet.*

As toasts go, it was old-fashioned and a little salty. Larry would have approved.

"God bless," Mickey mumbled.

He wasn't aware of falling asleep where he sat. Twi-light surrendered to night. The whiskey bottle nestled in his lap. No tiny creatures stirred in the woodwork because there was no woodwork. In any case, the management had been very good about spraying.

WAKE UP, KIDDO.

"I am awake."

Prove it. Open your eyes.

It wasn't until that moment that Mickey realized his eyes were closed. A faint glow shone on the other side of his eyelids. When he opened them, he saw that the glow was coming from the TV he had given his father for Christmas. Who had turned it on?

He started to get up, and the whiskey bottle rolled onto the floor with a clunk. Mickey didn't pay attention, though, because the TV was acting strange. The screen was filled with gray snow, but that wasn't strange in itself; he'd canceled the cable service the day before.

The strange part was that the fuzzy snow contained faint shapes. Mickey leaned down and took a closer look. He could make out the outline of a head, then two hands.

Don't turn it off.

He couldn't tell if the outline of the head had Larry's face, but this was definitely his father's voice. Which should have made Mickey jump back in alarm. Instead he was relieved, because it proved that he was dreaming.

"You're in the TV," Mickey said, raising his voice. If he pointed out the dream's absurdity, it would break the spell and he'd wake up.

I'm not in the TV. Don't talk crazy. I'm in limbo. They're letting me talk to you.

"They?"

God's people.

"You can see them?"

Not exactly. It's complicated. Just listen.

Mickey hesitated. His glance went down to the carpet, where the fallen whiskey bottle was dripping onto the floor. He could smell the sharp alcohol, and that was wrong. One thing Mickey knew for certain: he couldn't smell in his dreams.

"I'm turning this off," he mumbled.

He punched the power button on the remote, but the gray fuzz didn't disappear, or the shapes vaguely visible inside it. The hands now came into focus as they pressed up against the screen from the inside.

I want to help you.

"I don't need your help," Mickey said. He punched the remote several more times.

Forget the TV. The TV is just a way to reach you. You don't believe in psychics. This was more convenient.

Mickey shook his head. "You can't be my father. First, this limbo business is crap. Second—"

The hands turned to fists and started to bang against the screen. *Shut up. I didn't mean church limbo. It's more like a halfway house. Neither here nor there. Get it?*

"No. How could I?"

One thing about this bizarre apparition was convincing. Larry had always had a short fuse, and so did the voice. It started yelling louder.

Don't blow this, kiddo. Stop being a jerk and listen to me.

"All right, all right." Mickey sat down in the lounger again.

"I'm listening."

It's different here.

"I bet."

You don't understand. You can't. One minute I'm sitting in that chair, the one you're in. The next minute the whole room starts to disappear. The walls fade, and I start to go through the ceiling.

"You had a heart attack. You didn't feel that?"

Pain gets erased from your memory.

"Except when it doesn't," said Mickey doubtfully.

Don't interrupt. I kept going, up and up, until I could look down and see the whole earth, and everyone on it. I saw everybody on the daylight side and on the night side. I saw all ages, all races. It felt incredible, you cannot imagine.

"You didn't go into the light?" asked Mickey.

Nope. I wondered about that. I kept floating farther into

space, and the earth got smaller and smaller. I figured I must be getting closer to God.

"God's in outer space?" said Mickey.

The voice ignored this. It was getting more excited.

I kept looking around, but nothing. No God. No angels. Then I heard it. Can you imagine, kiddo? I heard the voice of God.

"What did he say?"

He didn't say anything. He was laughing.

"Who was he laughing at, you?"

No. He wasn't laughing at anybody. This laugh was everywhere. It filled the universe. It was pure joy.

The voice was now ecstatic, which wasn't like Larry at all. It made Mickey uneasy. It reminded him of the one time he had found his father crying, the day Mickey's mother had died. Anyway, what did Mickey care if God was laughing? Comedians make people laugh. It doesn't mean they're happy. Laughter is a reflex, like sneezing.

The voice had been quiet for a few seconds. Now it said, *Everyone should hear that sound. Kiddo, it would make all the difference.*

Mickey seriously doubted this, but he didn't interrupt again.

The voice sensed what Mickey was thinking.

I'm not fooling. Until the world laughs with God, nothing's going to change.

"Nothing's going to change anyway," Mickey said. He leaned down and picked up the fallen whiskey bottle from the floor. He considered taking a pull, then thought better of it.

"I'm glad you're okay, Dad," he said. "But I've gotta go. Have a nice limbo."

You don't believe me.

"What I believe is that I've taken a little detour into craziness. I'm going home to get some sleep. This has been a rough week."

Not for me.

"Congratulations."

This isn't the way to end, son. I have limited access. You need to listen. I can show you what to do. Then you'll hear it, too.

Mickey had already gotten up to leave.

"If God likes to laugh, here's a joke for him," he said. "A guy dies and goes to Hell. The Devil is giving him a tour, and they come across this ninety-year-old codger sitting on a park bench. He's smooching with a gorgeous twenty-year-old girl.

"The man says to the Devil, 'What's going on? This isn't Hell.'

"The Devil says, 'It is for the girl.'"

Ha, ha.

The voice sounded discouraged, but Mickey didn't

care. He couldn't imagine God laughing, unless he was laughing at the horrible mess human beings had made on earth, in which case it was a cruel laugh. Now the Devil, *he* might wear a grin, and for good reason.

Mickey suddenly felt a sadness in his chest. "I'm disappointed in you, Larry. You never used to preach at me. You made a lot of mistakes, but I gave you credit for one thing. You were never a hypocrite."

I can make up for everything, kiddo.

"Too late."

Mickey was already at the door. The fuzzy gray screen went black, and the room was plunged into darkness. His hand hesitated for just a second on the doorknob. The voice had warned him not to blow it. What if he just had?

2

THE NEXT MORNING PAYBACK JUMPED ON THE bed and started licking Mickey's face. Payback was a miniature Doberman. Mickey's ex-wife, Dolores, had named her Daisy, but after Mickey won the dog in the divorce, he renamed her Payback. That way, when people asked if the dog was a he or a she, Mickey could say, "Payback's a bitch." Anyway, Dolores might be gone, but the Doberman still loved him.

The dog began whining now, her eyes fixed on Mickey's face, demanding her morning walk. Or did she sense something different about him?

"Don't worry, baby," Mickey whispered in her ear. "Nothing's wrong. I promise." Payback whipped around and nipped his hand. She was the nervous type.

A few minutes later Mickey was leaning against the kitchen counter talking on the phone.

"Dump everything from my dad's apartment. Give it away. I don't want any of it."

Alicia, his agent, was on the other end. "What about photos, family stuff?"

"You go through it. I trust your judgment," said Mickey.

He took a sip of espresso. "You know, I've been thinking. I never do God jokes in my act."

"You want to start now?" Alicia sounded dubious. "What's going on with you?"

"Nothing." The eeriness of the previous night had faded. Whatever kind of delusion he'd gone through, it was temporary. Still, it would have been nice to talk to Larry, for real, one last time.

Alicia said, "Get some rest. Take a few days off. I can handle the predators."

"Thanks."

Payback was scratching at the door to get out. One side of the house, the side facing the ocean, was all French windows. Mickey put the dog's leash on, and they stepped out onto the beach. Payback barked frantically at the waves, as if they were thieves creeping in to steal the sand.

"You're a lunatic," said Mickey indulgently. It usually cheered him up to watch her madly charge into the surf, but today he felt glum and restless. He couldn't forget what Larry's voice had said. Not that any of it made sense.

Like almost everyone he knew, Mickey was allergic to God. What good ever came from believing in a deity who watched and did nothing about genocide, or AIDS, or children starving? God either didn't exist or was someone to be avoided.

That reminded Mickey of an old joke.

An atheist is swimming in the ocean when he sees the fin of a great white shark. In desperation he screams, "God, save me!"

All at once everything freezes, the heavens part, and a voice says, "Why should I save you? You don't believe in me."

The atheist has an idea. "Maybe you can get the shark to believe in you."

"Very well."

The heavens close again, and suddenly the shark is heading straight for the atheist. All of a sudden the shark stops and puts its fins together. It begins to pray.

The atheist is amazed. "It worked. This shark believes in God."

Just then he hears the shark muttering, "Oh Lord, make us thankful for the food we are about to receive."

Now Mickey noticed a stranger coming toward him. He wasn't a jogger or a swimmer or a fisherman, the types one usually sees at the beach. The stranger walked slowly and steadily in Mickey's direction. With the morning sun behind him he was only a silhouette. When he got closer, Mickey could make out a tall, olive-skinned man, maybe midthirties, with a spade beard, dressed in khakis and a blue shirt.

The man stopped directly in front of Mickey. "You have something for me," he said.

Mickey, taken aback, mumbled, "I don't think so."

"I'm usually right about these things," the man said. "Check your pockets."

His physical presence was intimidating—Mickey thought he looked like a Spanish conquistador without the armor—but his voice was reassuring.

"What would be in my pockets?" Mickey asked.

"A clue."

The conquistador waited. Clearly there was no brushing him off, so Mickey reached into the pockets of his jogging pants. He pulled out a folded piece of paper.

"Want me to read it for you?" the conquistador asked.

"No, I can do it."

As Mickey unfolded the paper, which had writing on one side, he said, "Mind telling me your name?"

"Francisco. I know yours. What does the note say?"

The fact that a perfect stranger would recognize him wasn't surprising to Mickey, so he read what was written on the piece of paper.

I tell many lies but am always believed
If the worst happens, I'll be greatly relieved
On the day you were born I poisoned your heart
I'll still be there on the day you depart.

The ominous riddle was penned in small, precise cursive. Francisco nodded, as if it was the clue he had been expecting.

"Now we know where to start," he said.

"Start what?" Mickey asked.

"The process," Francisco replied with some satisfaction. "You've been chosen. Not that it shows to look at you. That's okay. It almost never does."

Mickey shook his head. "I don't want to be chosen."

"Why not?"

Because I like my life the way it is, Mickey wanted to say. But he wasn't at all sure that was true, so he said instead, "My father just died. I'm not in a space where I can handle this."

"You mean Larry?" said Francisco. "Who do you think sent the note?"

Mickey's mouth went dry. "How do you know Larry?"

"Doesn't matter. You've received a clue. That's very, very unusual. You should be grateful." Francisco fixed

Mickey with a look. "Don't faint on me," he said. "Take some slow, deep breaths."

Mickey did as he was told. When he was sure he wasn't going to pass out, he said, "Are you going to take me away someplace?"

His trepidation made the tall stranger laugh. "No, nothing like that. First we're going to answer the riddle. Then we'll see where it takes us."

"I don't have an answer," said Mickey.

"You're too nervous to think straight," said Francisco. "Who wouldn't be?" He took the paper from Mickey's hands and considered it briefly. Then he wrote a word on it with a pencil from his pocket. When he handed the note back, the word turned out to be "Fear."

"That's the answer?" Mickey said.

Francisco nodded. "It fits every line." He recited the riddle, this time with the answer in place.

> Fear *tells many lies but is always believed*
> *If the worst happens,* fear *will be greatly relieved*
> *On the day you were born* fear *poisoned your heart*
> Fear *will still be there on the day you depart.*

"Don't look so disappointed," Francisco said. "We're going to make you fearless."

"I don't want to be," said Mickey, regretting that he had ever let the stranger give him the paper.

"You have to give the process a chance."

"Why? Frankly, the thing here that makes me the most nervous is you," said Mickey. At that moment he felt a nudge at his ankle, and he looked down to see Payback staring up at him. "She wants to go home. I'll see you."

Francisco shook his head. "You know what you remind me of? Somebody waiting to see the dentist. Most people in that waiting room don't show it, but they're all afraid. But when they come out, they're all smiles. Don't you want to come out all smiles?"

"I'm already Mr. Smiles," Mickey said. He felt a guilty twinge for dismissing the stranger's offer out of hand. "Nobody is totally fearless," he added.

"I am."

The claim could have sounded like an empty boast, but looking into Francisco's eyes, Mickey almost believed it. His eyes were as steady as the stars and totally calm. Francisco saw this moment of hesitation as an opening.

"Just try," he coaxed.

What could Mickey say? He couldn't very well run away—it would prove the stranger's point about being afraid. And Alicia had told him to take a few days off. He might as well play along.

✄

"THE FIRST THING," said Francisco, "is that fear is a liar. Just like the riddle says."

Mickey found it a little hard to hear him, because they were standing on the shoulder of the highway that ran beside the beach. Six lanes of cars and trucks roared by.

"Why are we here?" asked Mickey.

Instead of answering, Francisco said, "What would happen if you walked into traffic right now?"

"I'd be killed."

"See, that's a lie. Try it."

"Are you crazy?"

Francisco shook his head. "Step off the curb. You're safe. It's a parking lane." Two cars were parked in front of them, with a space between their bumpers wide enough to walk between.

Mickey stepped off the curb, but he felt uneasy. "Where is this going?"

"Don't ask questions. Keep walking."

Mickey edged closer to the stream of traffic. He stopped at the edge of the parked cars.

"Go on," Francisco urged. "Walk around to the front door as if you were going to unlock it." Mickey did as he was told. "Now face the traffic, and walk into it."

This guy is *crazy,* Mickey thought.

"You'll never be fearless until you try," said Francisco.

What the hell. Mickey waited until he saw a gap in the traffic, and then he stepped into the road. As he braced himself for another step he heard the sound of a blaring horn. Out of nowhere a panel truck was barreling down on him. Instantly he jumped back, and the van whooshed by. The driver glared at him as he passed.

Mickey hurried back to the curb. "So what was that supposed to prove?"

"It proved that you couldn't get yourself killed. You jumped back just in time. Why? Because your body acts on instinct. Where there's danger, it moves to escape."

Mickey's heart was pounding from his close call, and it was hard to listen to what the tall stranger was saying. "I still could have been killed," he insisted.

"No, that's just your fear talking. Try again. Make yourself walk into traffic. You won't get hit. Your body won't let you. It knows how to take care of itself."

Mickey certainly wasn't going to step into traffic again. But he imagined himself edging into the stream of cars, and knew Francisco was right. The impulse to jump back would be overwhelming.

"What if you're right," he said. "I don't see what this has to do with fear being a liar."

Francisco said, "Fear tells you that you aren't safe.
But you are. Thinking that you aren't safe is an illusion.
If you believe in an illusion, you're buying into a lie."

Francisco didn't give Mickey a chance to object.
"You're going to tell me all the reasons I'm wrong," he
went on. "Try to think of why I might be right."

This was harder than it looked. Suddenly Mickey's
mind was filled with all the things he worried about
most. Cancer. The drunk driver swerving into Mickey's
lane and hitting him head-on. The gangbanger on a
spree, spraying the street with bullets. Carjacking. Home
invasion. He forced his mind to stop.

"See what you're doing?" said Francisco. "You're
imagining things."

"They're not so imaginary," said Mickey.

"Yes, they are. Fear's main tactic is to make illusion
seem real. But imagined pain isn't the same as real pain.
Imagined death isn't real death. When you give in to
fear, you are either projecting into the future or reliving
the past. Here and now, you are safe. While fear is trying
to convince you that it's real, what's really happening is
that you lose touch with the present. The world turns
into one big dentist's waiting room with everyone anticipating the next thing that hurts."

"Sometimes the dentist does hurt," Mickey said.

"So you're saying that fear helps it hurt less? I don't

think so. If everybody is afraid in the waiting room but only five percent wind up feeling pain in the chair, then fear is pointless ninety-five percent of the time. Fear is a terrible predictor of the future. In fact, nothing is as unreliable as fear, and yet people rely on it over and over again."

Francisco saw that he was making an impression. "That's good. Your mind is beginning to relax," he said.

"I don't know," said Mickey doubtfully. "There's still that five percent."

"If the local weatherman was right only five percent of the time," said Francisco, "he'd get fired tomorrow. It's time to fire your fear. Let's go."

He started to walk away from the highway. In the near distance a new row of beach condos was going up. "We need something from that construction site," said Francisco.

After a moment he pointed to Mickey's pockets. "Read the second line of the riddle."

Mickey pulled out the paper. "If the worst happens, I'll be greatly relieved."

"That's how fear works," said Francisco. "Anytime one of your fears comes true, you give fear the credit for having protected you until that moment. Which only encourages you to spend your whole life anticipating disaster. "

Mickey was feeling more relaxed around the tall stranger as they walked side by side with Payback trotting ahead. He still felt he was playing along, but Francisco could be right. A part of his mind—a small fragment—felt like it might be thawing.

"You're telling me that I should never be afraid?" he said. "That's unrealistic."

"Is it? Here's a story for you. A young woman goes to her doctor to get a checkup. 'I'm deathly afraid of cancer,' she says. 'Are you sure I'm okay?' The doctor says, 'Absolutely. Your tests are clean. You don't have cancer.'

"But she's still sure she does, so a few weeks later the woman goes back. The doctor examines her again, and again he says she has nothing to worry about. She doesn't have cancer.

"This goes on for years. Every few months the woman goes to see the doctor, certain that she has cancer, and every time she doesn't.

"Finally she's eighty, and when she goes for her next checkup the doctor says, 'I'm terribly sorry. I have bad news. You have cancer.'

"The woman throws up her hands. 'I told you so.'"

It wasn't a story you could laugh at, but Mickey gave a wry smile.

"You get the point?" said Francisco. "Just because something bad happens doesn't prove that your fear was right. Fear will never stop trying to convince you. But when you choose to stop being convinced, you'll be fearless."

By this point they had reached the construction site. Since it was a weekend, no one was around. Francisco went over to a dumpster full of discarded scraps and rummaged through it. After a moment he pulled out a long wooden plank.

"Here we go," he said, laying it on the ground. "How wide would you say this board is, six inches?"

"About," said Mickey.

"And how long, eight feet?"

"Yeah."

"Let's see you walk it without falling off."

Mickey stepped onto one end of the narrow plank and walked to the other.

"Easy?" said Francisco.

Mickey nodded.

"You're sure? Try again."

Mickey walked back.

Picking up the board, Francisco headed for the nearest condo block, located a fire escape, and began to ascend.

"Follow me."

This particular block was almost finished, and when they got to the roof Francisco looked around. They were five stories up. The ocean view reached south to Santa Monica and north to Malibu. Instead of taking it in, Francisco walked to the far edge of the roof, where there was a gap between this building and the next. He laid the plank down. It barely crossed the gap.

"All right, walk it again," he said.

Mickey peered down nervously into the yawning fifty-foot drop. "I can't," he said.

"But you just did. Twice. When we were on the ground, there was no problem."

"This is different."

"Why?"

Francisco regarded him for a moment. "What's stopping you is fear. Rationally, you should have no trouble walking the same board you walked before. But fear tells you that you can't. Why believe it?"

"Because if I fall, I'll break my neck," said Mickey.

"Fear pushes you to confuse what you imagine with what's real," Francisco said. Without warning he stepped out onto the plank. When he was suspended over the middle, he turned around.

"My balance is no better than yours. Now watch."

He did a quick spin, and then bounced lightly on the board, which bent and creaked under his weight. Watching him made Mickey almost nauseous with anxiety.

"Stop that. Come back," he cried.

Francisco complied. When he was back beside Mickey, he regarded him. "It made you afraid to watch me. Isn't that strange? You weren't in danger. You weren't even in imagined danger."

"I was afraid for you," said Mickey. It seemed like a reasonable thing to say, but Francisco was shaking his head.

"See how fear spreads everywhere? It even reaches into situations that have nothing to do with you, and every space it seeps into becomes full of danger."

They crossed the roof and headed back down the fire escape. Neither said anything until they were back on terra firma.

"That's enough for one day," said Francisco. "Should I find you again? Your choice."

Mickey was guarded. "What's next?"

"Today we flirted with fear. Tomorrow we get serious about it. Maybe add a touch of terror. How does that sound?"

"Awful."

"I'll tell you what's awful. Read the last two lines of your riddle," Francisco said.

Mickey took out the paper and read.

On the day you were born I poisoned your heart
I'll still be there on the day you depart

When Mickey had finished, the tall stranger said, "I can make you a promise. If you don't go through with this process, you'll be afraid until the day you die."

"Really?"

"Really."

On that note Francisco departed. Mickey soon realized that he had forgotten to ask what this all had to do with God laughing. He was pretty sure there had to be a connection somewhere. Larry wouldn't sabotage him. And if he had? Death means never having to say you're sorry.

He could hear Alicia scolding him. "Don't steal material, Mickey. You're better than that."

3

ICKEY HAD TO ADMIT THAT FRANCISCO WAS
quite remarkable. What did he have? Magnetism,
charisma? But once Francisco had gone, their
encounter quickly faded. By the next day the whole
thing seemed like a waste of time. His goal in life wasn't
to be fearless. Why should it be?

When Payback jumped on the bed to wake him up,
Mickey didn't take her for a walk. He had decided to
avoid the beach, in case Francisco might be waiting there
for him.

He felt restless all morning. He flipped through some
magazines, but that didn't take long. And he was too jit-
tery to sit in front of the TV. Around noon the phone
rang. Mickey jumped, even though he had no reason to
be spooked.

It was his sister in Atlanta. "I'm just calling to see if
you need anything," she said.

"What would I need?"

"I don't know."

His sister's name was Janet, and she and Mickey didn't talk very often. When their parents were divorced, brother and sister were split up. Half the family stayed in Chicago, and the other half moved to Atlanta. Mickey, who remained behind with his father, didn't see Janet unless he was visiting his mother, and that had only happened for one week every summer. He wasn't surprised when she'd decided not to come out for the funeral.

Janet said, "I keep thinking he suffered. They say that nothing hurts like a heart attack. It's like having a truck drive over your chest."

"Sis, don't."

"You're sure he didn't feel anything?"

"No, it happened like *that*." Mickey snapped his fingers.

"But we can't be sure, can we?" Her voice quivered. "Dad could have been lying there for a while, all alone and in pain. He might have been going through hell."

"It doesn't do any good imagining things."

"I guess you're right." Janet paused, pulling herself together. "I wish I had your certainty," she said.

What did that mean? It reminded Mickey that the two of them didn't know each other very well. When his career took off, his sister had never called to offer congratulations. She didn't use the free tickets Mickey sent to her when he was on tour or a new movie opened.

"Do you think I'm funny?" he asked.

"What?"

The question had come out of left field. Mickey didn't know why he asked it. But it only took a few seconds for Janet to reply.

"I grew up with you," she said. "You never told jokes. You weren't the class clown or a jerk. Mom and Dad's divorce changed you."

"Meaning that I suddenly became a jerk?"

"Don't get defensive, Mickey. That's not what I mean. You just changed. You wanted to be funny all the time. It was weird, that's all."

"Really? So to you I'm not funny. I'm a . . . what? A kid brother who turned into a motormouth?"

"Now you're mad."

Mickey didn't deny it.

"You asked me a question, Mickey. I just thought we shouldn't be so distant with each other," said Janet.

"Sorry. It's been crazy stressful around here the last few days."

Janet accepted this peace offering. She mumbled that she was sorry, too, and hung up.

Suddenly the big, airy house felt like a shoebox. Mickey wandered out onto the beach deck. At the far end a man was sitting in one of the low white lounge chairs Mickey used for sunning. It was Francisco.

"Things like that will start happening more now," he said, not getting up.

"What are you talking about?" Mickey snapped. He skipped any friendly greeting.

"Once the process starts, you open a door. Then the unexpected peeks in."

"Screw the process," said Mickey sourly.

Francisco wasn't offended. "Poor Mickey," he murmured. He took a moment longer to enjoy the brilliant expanse of ocean spread out before them, then he got up.

"We need to go in your car, and you need to bring a joke with you. That shouldn't be a problem, right?"

Still agitated by the conversation with his sister, Mickey decided he wouldn't mind some company. "Okay," he said.

A moment later they were speeding along the Coast Highway. Francisco pointed to Sunset Boulevard when the turnoff came.

"Wherever you're taking me, it's cool," said Mickey. "But just so you know, I'm not what you think."

"Which is what?" said Francisco.

"Scared of life. Worried. Anxious."

"All right."

"You don't believe me."

Francisco shrugged. "What I believe doesn't matter. You're taking what I said too personally. Everyone is born into fear and almost everyone stays there until they die."

"What makes you special?"

"When you aren't living in fear, you see the truth. It becomes obvious."

"If you say so," Mickey muttered. He was keeping his eyes on the road as Sunset made broad sweeping curves through lush neighborhoods. Francisco didn't direct him to turn off anywhere.

"Did you bring a joke like I asked?" Francisco said.

"What kind do you want?"

"A dog joke."

Mickey shrugged.

"A man walks into a bar with his dog. He says to the bartender, 'My dog Fido can talk. If you give me a free drink, I'll prove it.'

"The bartender is curious, so he pours the man a drink. 'Can you really talk?' he says to the dog.

"'Indubitably I can,' the dog replies.

"The bartender is so impressed, he takes out some money. 'Here's five dollars,' he says to the dog. 'Go across the street and talk for my friend Paddy.' The dog takes the money and leaves.

"A few minutes later his owner comes out of the bar, and what does he see but his dog humping another dog in the gutter. He's shocked.

"'Fido,' he exclaims, 'you never did this before!'

"The dog says, 'I never had five dollars before.'"

It wasn't the greatest joke, but when Francisco didn't laugh, Mickey grew irritated. "I get paid big money to tell jokes," he said.

Francisco cut him short. "Turn there," he said, pointing to a house on the left.

"You know these people?" Mickey asked.

"No," Francisco replied calmly.

Mickey felt nervous about turning into a stranger's driveway. Once they were parked, he followed Francisco, who didn't go to the front door but went around the back. After a few yards Mickey could hear loud barking. When he rounded the corner he saw two German shepherds, who began barking even more furiously. They lunged frantically at the two strangers, straining at the chains around their necks.

"This is wrong. We have to leave," Mickey said with alarm. He expected the owners of the house to come charging out at any minute.

"Come closer," said Francisco.

"No way."

He wasn't normally afraid of dogs, but these two were big and dangerous. Their fangs were bared now, and they were making a deafening noise. Mickey could feel his heart pounding.

Francisco plucked at his sleeve. "They want to hear your dog joke," he said. He pulled Mickey within a foot of the dogs, who became frenzied. "Go ahead."

"A man walks into a bar," Mickey began. He could hardly get the words out. One of the dogs began to foam at the corners of its mouth.

"This is nuts," Mickey screamed. He pulled away and ran back around the corner of the house, heading for the car.

To his surprise, Francisco didn't object. He followed, while behind them the dogs kept barking madly.

"You would have calmed down in a few minutes," Francisco said.

"I doubt it."

They got into the car and backed down the driveway. Mickey was in no mood to listen until they were back on the road and well clear of the house.

Francisco said, "I did that to show you that thinking you're not living in fear is deceptive. Fear is your silent partner, and it jumps out when you least expect it."

"I don't need a stupid stunt like that," Mickey grumbled. "Those dogs were killers. Anybody would have been scared."

"Their owners? Are they scared?"

"They don't count."

"You're not catching on. People get used to fear, and

they mistake that for overcoming fear. The owners are used to their dogs, but if they came out one day and found two alligators instead, that would change in a hurry," said Francisco.

Mickey was still rattled. "You're right, I'm not catching on, because for some amazing reason I don't keep surprise alligators around."

"Stop resisting. I'm trying to get you to look inside yourself," Francisco said. "Even when you don't notice it, fear has you in its grasp. Anytime it wants to, it can jump you, and you'll be powerless to resist."

Mickey kept brooding, but at some level he was taking this in. The tall stranger certainly believed what he was saying. And on his terms he made sense. Maybe it was time to loosen up a little. "Just show me where this is going," Mickey said.

Francisco said, "Imagine that your worst enemy comes over to your house. He sits down in the living room, and no matter what you do, he won't go away. Day after day he refuses to leave. What do you do? You begin to ignore him. You pretend he's not there."

"I'd call the police," Mickey pointed out.

"Stop fighting me," said Francisco.

"All right, all right."

"Your home isn't your home if there's an enemy living there. It doesn't matter if you toss a drop cloth over him, or if you decide to completely redecorate the place. Until you figure out a way to make your enemy leave, you'll never feel safe."

Francisco made his points matter-of-factly. Now he leaned into his next words. "The world is your home, and it is safe. God created it that way. But fear crept in. Big problem. Nobody feels safe anymore."

"Amen to that," Mickey muttered.

"As long as you live in fear, the world is a threat. If that doesn't matter to you, okay. But living that way you'll never know the joy of your own soul," said Francisco.

Mickey grimaced. "Are you always this upbeat? I'm not getting a sugar rush."

Francisco chuckled. "You think I should lighten up?"

"It wouldn't hurt."

Francisco looked out the window at the perfect blue sky. When he didn't resume talking, Mickey was relieved. There was too much to absorb, and his stomach felt faintly queasy.

On the day you were born I poisoned your heart.

How depressing. It seemed like a month since he'd run into Larry's ghost, or whatever it was, in the TV. And God still wasn't laughing, at least not so that Mickey could hear.

Janet was right, though. After their parents divorced,

he had turned into a joker. But she didn't understand why. Mickey hadn't been sad or lonely. He had just wanted to be happy, and he had figured out, as early as fifteen, that nobody else could do that for him. Hearing other people laugh was pure pleasure, and the only comfort he could give himself.

"Want to hear a joke about the end of the world?" Mickey asked.

Francisco turned his head. "Sure."

"A little old lady goes into a restaurant. She eats a salad. Then she says to the waiter, 'I'll have an ice cream sundae.'

"'I'm sorry to tell you, madam,' says the waiter, 'but in five minutes the world is coming to an end.'

"The little old lady thinks for a second, then she says, 'In that case, heavy on the whipped cream.'"

"NOW FOR A dose of abject terror," Francisco told Mickey. "It's going to be intense. Don't fall apart on me." His warning would have been more believable if they were somewhere else.

"Here?" said Mickey. "This is a toy store."

"Just wait."

Francisco was looking around as if he expected to find something. After a minute he found what he was looking for: a mother and a little girl of around three. The mother was bending down to show her daughter a baby doll in a pink cardboard package. Nothing could be more innocent.

Then the mother's cell phone rang. She pulled it out of her purse and answered it.

"Hello? What? You're breaking up." She looked frustrated and began to walk away.

"Here's where it happens," Francisco said in a low voice.

The little girl, mesmerized by the doll, didn't notice that her mother had stepped away. Now the mother was out of sight around a corner, and her child still hadn't noticed. Thirty seconds passed before she looked up. Her chin began to quiver.

Mickey knew what was coming. Not seeing her mother, the little girl looked around for a moment, and began to cry. The doll was forgotten. She started to run, unfortunately in the wrong direction.

Mickey winced. There was no mistaking the child's distress, but there was nothing he could do. If he ran over to her, it would only frighten her more. Just then the mother reappeared from around the corner.

"It's okay, Mommy's back." She picked up her little girl and rocked her in her arms. "I didn't go away, silly. You don't need to be scared."

But anyone could see that the little girl was still par-
alyzed with fear. She didn't let up screaming and sob-
bing. The mother looked embarrassed and quickly
walked away.

"Abject terror," said Francisco. "I never get used
to it."

"I don't want to sound like an insensitive jerk," said
Mickey, "but—"

"But things like this happen every day. I know. To
you it's a small moment. But she's never going to forget
it." Francisco turned and faced Mickey. "You have memo-
ries like that, too."

"I suppose."

"Can you see how important that is?"

Before Mickey could answer, Francisco's tone softened.
He put his hand on Mickey's shoulder. "This isn't about
who's afraid and who's not. Fear is one of the strongest
layers of illusion. It's like a fog bank inside each person.
But if you could pierce the fog, you'd see that something
incredible lies on the other side. Something you can't
even imagine."

Suddenly an idea hit Mickey. "Is that what my father
saw? Was that what he was trying to tell me about?"

"Did your father love you?" Francisco asked.

Mickey was startled. "I guess so. I'm not sure."

"He absolutely loves you now."

Francisco sounded so sure. How did he know?

Mickey said, "Is my dad talking to you now?" He knew about psychics who communicated with the dead. He'd surfed past them on cable channels late at night.

Francisco hesitated. "You're asking the wrong question," he said. "Talking to the dead assumes that they *are* dead. They aren't. Death is life on another frequency. The music doesn't end just because someone can't hear it."

He could see that Mickey wasn't satisfied.

"Everything you want to know will become clear," he said. "Let the process unfold. If I told you in advance you might know the truth, but you wouldn't own it. I want you to own it."

Without waiting for Mickey's response, Francisco headed for the door. Then he paused for a moment.

"Could you feel that little girl's terror?" he asked.

"I guess so."

"I think everybody can. You saw a moment that girl will never forget. She'll just get older and hide it from sight."

Mickey felt a shiver. "What did we say about lightening up?"

They walked through the parking lot until they found Mickey's car. Francisco leaned against the passenger door staring at the ground. Quietly he said, "I know this is hard for you. That little girl's terror made you feel your own."

"Jesus, give it a rest!" Mickey glared into Francisco's fathomless eyes. "Whatever," he muttered, climbing into the driver's seat.

Once they were on the Coast Highway again, Mickey began to calm down. He thought about Larry, and the possibility that his father loved him more than he could show. A memory came to him.

When he was twelve Mickey had been sent away to summer camp. He'd been to camp before, and he looked forward to what he had loved the summer before: campfires, ghost stories, canoe raids on the girls' camp across the lake. But the bus didn't go north where the lakes were; it went south.

When Mickey got off, the first thing he saw was a huge man in army fatigues, screaming at the kids to line up as they stepped off the bus. Veins stood out on the man's bull neck; his face was purple. Mickey's legs shook with terror. Nobody had told him he was being sent off to a new camp that summer. Mickey's father hadn't even hinted at a reason why his son might be sent here.

As kids do, Mickey adapted. He shaved his head and made friends in the barracks. He learned how to make hospital corners on his bed and not to complain about push-ups at dawn. To his surprise, by the time the bus brought him home, Mickey wasn't angry. He was proud that he had toughened up; he was glad his father had wanted him to become a man's man.

But he could never answer one question: why did his father want to scare him so damn much?

Was Larry trying to make amends now?

"No debt in the universe goes unpaid," said Francisco. He seemed to find it easy to tune in on Mickey's thoughts. "That includes good debts," he added with a smile.

Mickey shook off the memory of that boot camp for kids. He glanced over at Francisco. "I'm going to tell you the last joke that made my dad laugh.

"A Wall Street lawyer is desperate to get promoted. He works his tail off, but nobody in the firm notices him. One night he can't take it anymore, so he calls on the Devil.

"'Okay, I can fix it so you make partner,' the Devil says. 'But in return I want the souls of your wife, your children, your grandchildren, and all your friends.'

"The lawyer thinks for a second. 'What's the catch?'"

A flicker of amusement crossed Francisco's face. He looked thoughtful. "A lot of your jokes are about things you might be afraid of if you didn't laugh at them," he remarked.

Mickey wished the man would just laugh and not try to find the meaning of everything. Francisco picked up on this.

"You think I'm grim. I'm not," he said. "I'm leading you out of the darkness where I found you."

Mickey had expected something conciliatory. This wasn't it.

"What do you mean by darkness?" he asked.

"The place where you feel lost and alone."

Mickey's face twitched nervously. "Am I still in that place?" he said.

Francisco nodded.

4

WHATEVER THE PROCESS WAS, IT CERTAINLY wasn't calming. Mickey hadn't been home two hours before he felt like jumping out of his skin. He paced back and forth, then reached for the phone and dialed.

One ring. Two. Three.

He was calling his ex-wife, Dolores. When she answered, he would say, "I think Larry's watching out for me. I'm not drunk or weirded out or anything. I just have this feeling, and I wanted somebody to know."

On the fifth ring her voice mail came on. Mickey left his message. It wasn't that Dolores would react well to it, but she was the only person Mickey knew who wouldn't tell people he had lost it. Dolores had issues with him, but disloyalty wasn't one of them.

Now what?

All the talk about fear had upset him, and he couldn't shake it. He had no appetite. His skin felt cold. Being alone wasn't helping.

Mickey reached for his car keys. A moment later he was down in the garage choosing between the Escalade and his old Porsche, a cream two-seater with red leather interiors. It was the first luxury he'd splurged on once he was sure that his success wasn't a mirage. He chose the Porsche and backed out of the garage.

There was one place in the world he could go to. One place where he was king, and fear meant nothing.

HEADS TURNED WHEN Mickey walked into a shabby bar in North Hollywood. The Miller Lite sign over the window was thirty years old, and looked it. A mirrored disco ball hung forlornly over an empty dance floor.

Mickey wasn't two steps through the door before the owner came running up.

"Mickey, is that you? I can't believe it."

"Hey, Sol. You still have amateur night?"

"Sure, of course. Every Friday. You remember that? It must be fifteen years."

Sol was a retired Hollywood extra who used to get plenty of work in the old days, when movies were movies. "Look at this face," he'd say. "I can play Italians, Jews, Indians, you name it. I once had a callback to play Geronimo. It's the nose. The camera loves my nose."

"Remember my first joke?" Mickey said. He pointed at the beer sign and recited. "You know why vampires hang out in this bar? They can come in any time and ask for a Blood Lite."

Sol shook his head and laughed. "Yeah. You bombed big-time that night."

But not for long. Mickey had been nineteen at the time, a college dropout in torn jeans and a Grateful Dead T-shirt. He didn't know much, but he knew in his heart he could be funny. An ad in a throwaway newspaper said there was an open microphone on Friday nights at a North Hollywood dive. Turned out, it drew lots of comics from hell, and Mickey.

Now he looked around. About a third of the tables were populated.

"How about I do half a set?" Mickey asked.

Sol's face fell. "It's not Friday, Mickey. The place is dead. You should have told me."

Then it hit Sol that one of the biggest comics in the business was in his establishment. He shouted to the bartender to give Mickey anything he wanted, and then Sol disappeared. He came back a minute later with a microphone and a stand. Mickey took it and walked to the far end of the room. He tapped the mike. Customers looked up. Then they did a double take.

"Folks, this is for Sol, who gave me my start."

While Mickey did his set people kept using their cell phones to take pictures and call their friends. Mickey was six jokes in when new faces began to appear in the audience. After half an hour the place was packed. They were laughing hysterically. They adored him.

Mickey knew he was only there as a distraction, but at least it was working. He was feeling high; the one-liners were rolling off his tongue like butter. He almost turned the two big guard dogs into part of his act. Instead, he riffed on religion.

"I just came back from touring the Midwest. Any Lutherans here tonight?"

A hand shot up in the back.

"Okay, I'll talk slower."

He was on such a roll that he could have told the gags in Urdu and nobody would have cared.

"My grandpa's the most religious man I know. He says if God had meant for man to fly, he would have given us tickets." That one dated back to junior high. Mickey could dredge them up from as far back as he wanted. His mind was churning one-liners so fast his mouth couldn't keep up.

"People say God isn't listening, but he answers knee-mail.

"You all know about the Golden Rule: Those who have the gold, rule.

"The problem with fundamentalists is that ninety-nine percent of them are giving the rest a bad name."

It had to end eventually. He wanted to finish on a joke that would make the whole room go, *"Awww."* A warm and fuzzy.

"I went to Catholic school as a kid. One day I was in the lunch line, and there was this pile of apples. The nun in charge wagged her finger. 'Just take one. God is watching.'

"So I took an apple, and the line moved along. At the next table there was this pile of chocolate chip cookies. I didn't know what to do.

"'Pssst,' the kid behind me whispered. 'Take all you want. God's watching the apples.'"

Mickey got his *"Awww."* And a huge round of applause.

When he came off, Sol ran up and hugged him with an old man's tears in his eyes. They sat at the bar while the crowd mobbed Mickey for autographs. Nobody wanted to leave without buying him a drink.

Francisco was the farthest thing from his mind.

It would have been a perfect night, except that when he walked back to his car, Mickey found a parking ticket stuck on the windshield. He couldn't believe it, and then he began to fume. What kind of idiot cop gives parking tickets after midnight?

But when he reached over to pull it off the windshield, he saw it wasn't a ticket after all. It was a folded sheet of white paper. Mickey felt a shiver as he opened it.

I'm keeping your secret, you're paying my price
You know if you don't, I'll stop being nice
Protection is worth it, wouldn't you say?
Life is so empty when you don't get your way

Who am I?

Mickey wadded up the note and hurled it into the night. He felt sick. Francisco was watching. And the second riddle was obviously intended to upset Mickey. Why else would it suggest blackmail?

MICKEY LOST SOME sleep obsessing over the riddle. He was still in bed at ten the next morning when Dolores called him back.

"Are you sure you're okay? That was a strange message you left," she said.

"You know me, I'm always cool," said Mickey.

Dolores laughed. "Yeah, I know you. That's why I called."

This wasn't a put-down. Dolores had been instantly attracted to Mickey when they first met. He was almost famous by then, which gave him a certain bravado around beautiful women. Before that, a tall, willowy brunette like her would have been way out of his league. Dolores liked his boldness during their courtship, and for a long time afterward.

"What makes you think Larry's watching over you from Heaven?" she asked.

"I dunno," Mickey said evasively. "I was in a strange mood. Maybe it was because of the way he died, all alone with nobody around."

Dolores knew about his father's death, but she lived in Connecticut now. She hadn't been able to come to the funeral on such short notice.

"Mickey, I don't want to get into a whole thing with you," she said. "But you don't even believe in an afterlife. You don't go to church. You're the prototype for 'Life sucks, and then you die.' If you think Larry is watching over you, something has happened."

"Not really."

"Truth?"

"Okay, okay." Mickey took a deep breath. "I think Larry came to me after he died. He had a message for me."

"Really?"

"You think I'm nuts."

"Maybe."

Dolores said this in an even tone, as if the situation could go one way or the other. She had always been extremely reasonable. "What was the message?"

"God is laughing."

A pause. Mickey had no idea what was running through her mind. "What does that mean?" Dolores asked.

"It means that everything's okay. Larry wants the human race to know that we worry too much."

"That's nice. But since when does dying make you smart all of a sudden?"

Was this Dolores being reasonable or trying to be funny? Mickey wanted to let the whole thing go. But now that he had opened up to someone, he couldn't stop.

"Larry really got to me," he said. "I mean, God has always been a scary bastard. I figured that out when I was a kid. Maybe he doesn't create all the terrible things in the world, but he doesn't lift a finger to stop them."

"I don't see it that way," said Dolores. "Not that you ever asked me."

Which was true. It had never occurred to Mickey that she had any interest in God, any more than he did.

"How do you see it?" he asked.

"You don't want to know."

"Yeah, I do. I'm trying to tell you that I'm really thinking things over."

Something in his tone—a hint of candor, a rare show of vulnerability—made Dolores go on. "I think the world had a chance to be perfect, but then we blew it. We're living in the crap of all our past mistakes. The garbage has piled up so high we can't see over it. We did the crime, now we're doing the time. "

Mickey was dismayed to hear this. "I had no idea you were so bummed out," he said.

"I'm not. I'm a realist. I haven't believed in Adam and Eve since I was sixteen, and I don't blame anything on the Devil. That's not the point, though, is it? A fallen world would have hit bottom by now. We just keep falling. But for some reason I keep thinking maybe we've still got a chance."

"You honestly believe that?"

He could feel her hesitation at the other end. "Mickey, I don't feel comfortable talking about this with you."

"Why not?"

"You really want to know?"

"Absolutely."

Dolores sounded very sober now. "You're a comedian, and comedians tend to be ruthless. Anything for a laugh. I never know when you might put me down. So I decided a long time ago to keep the really private stuff to myself."

Mickey wanted to remind her about the idyllic few years they had had together. Before he could open his mouth, his mind flashed on Dolores writing in her journal and shutting it the minute Mickey came into the room. Dolores donating a thousand dollars to Mother Teresa's orphanage in India, and Mickey reminding her that she was spending his money. Dolores talking about Kabbalah and the look on her face when Mickey teased her about it in front of their friends.

"I didn't know you felt that way," he said, feebly.

"It's all behind us now, Mickey. It's okay." Dolores's tone softened. "Sounds like you're asking yourself some tough questions. Maybe you're even changing, Mickey."

They chatted for a few more minutes. After Dolores hung up, Mickey sat back. He could have sunk into a major depression then and there, but the doorbell rang. Mickey jumped up to answer it, grateful for the distraction. When he opened the door, he found Francisco on the doorstep.

"You look shell-shocked," Francisco remarked. He stepped inside without being invited.

"My ex," Mickey mumbled.

"She always saw through you. That was a good thing, only you didn't see it that way." Francisco sounded casual; he didn't wait for a reaction. "You have the second riddle?"

"I threw it away. It bothered me."

Francisco shrugged. "I brought a copy. So, it offended you?"

"It felt like some kind of demand for hush money. How else should I feel?"

"That's entirely up to you."

Francisco pulled out a piece of paper from his cargo pants. He wore the same outfit every time, khaki pants and a blue work shirt. It made him look austere, the way a monk would look if he cast off his robes.

He read aloud.

I'm keeping your secret, you're paying my price
You know if you don't, I'll stop being nice

Francisco looked up. "Your secret is that you think you're nothing, a nobody." He went back to reading.

Protection is worth it, wouldn't you say?
Life is so empty when you don't get your way

Who am I?

"Protection isn't hush money in this case," said Francisco. "It's your defenses, the walls you live behind."

"I don't feel too protected right this minute," Mickey grumbled. He hadn't shaken off what Dolores had said to him, and now Francisco was back.

The tall man refolded the riddle and handed it to Mickey. "I put the answer on the back, in case you're interested."

Mickey turned the slip of paper over and read a single word: "Ego."

"I don't get it," he said. "But before you explain anything, let's get out of here."

"Fine. There's someplace I need to take you anyway," said Francisco.

Mickey didn't pretend that this was good news, but he led the way down to the garage. In a minute they were in the Escalade, heading down the Coast Highway.

"Yesterday's riddle was about fear, today's is about ego," said Francisco. "Ask yourself, why would people choose to be afraid? Fear makes the world feel scary and unsafe. If that's only an illusion, why hold on to it?"

"I don't know."

Francisco tapped the shirt pocket where Mickey had put the piece of paper. "Ego. Your ego makes believe that you are in control, that you will get what you want. After a while, your fear is put out of your mind. You have a self-image to keep up, after all. You need other people to believe in you. There's money, status, possessions, and a family to acquire. As long as ego keeps holding out the carrot and creating constant drama, you never have to face what lies below the surface."

"Not everybody has a big ego," Mickey protested. He assumed that Francisco had been referring to him.

Francisco shook his head. "It's not a matter of whether your ego is inflated or not. We need a demonstration. That's where we're heading."

There was nothing more to say for the next few miles. Francisco asked Mickey to turn off the highway at Santa Monica, where they parked in a municipal lot. Then he walked them over to a nearby pedestrian mall.

"Okay," Francisco said. "I want you to go up to people and tell them a joke. That's your specialty, so it shouldn't be too hard."

"That's all?" Mickey said warily.

"That's all."

Mickey offered no resistance. He spotted a thirty-something woman in expensive sunglasses. She was window-shopping and she looked approachable. Mickey walked up to her.

"Excuse me," he said. "I'm telling free jokes today to cheer people up. Want to hear one?"

The woman was a little startled, but she said yes.

Mickey let his mind toss out a joke at random. "A man goes to his doctor for a rectal exam. The doctor says, 'That's strange. You have a strawberry up your ass. But don't worry. I have cream for that.'"

The woman in the sunglasses screwed up her face. "That's gross," she said. She started to back away.

"Wait," said Mickey, but she had turned away and quickly crossed the street. He was stunned. That was an awful joke. Why had he come up with it?

Twenty feet away Francisco nodded encouragement. "Find someone else," he said.

Mickey looked around. An older couple was heading toward him. They looked easygoing, so he approached.

"I'd like to tell you a joke," he said.

They were flustered. "Are we on TV?" the woman asked, gazing around.

"No, why?"

"We know who you are. You're famous," the man said. "Why would you talk to us?"

Mickey felt a surge of confidence. "It's okay, folks. I just feel like telling a joke," he said. "And I'd be glad to sign an autograph afterwards."

The woman was smiling now, feeling reassured. "What a treat," she said. She started rummaging in her purse for a pen and paper.

"Great. This is just for you," said Mickey. "What do you get when you cross a mouse and a lion? A mouse that nobody picks on."

The couple had been smiling with anticipation. Now the smiles gave way to embarrassed disappointment.

"Wait," Mickey said hurriedly. "That was just a test."

The couple looked hopeful again. Mickey felt sweat under his armpits. He flipped through his mental index.

What's red and not there? No tomatoes.

A pun is its own reword.

What did the finger say to the thumb? I'm in glove with you.

Where was this garbage coming from? "Just hold on," Mickey said. He forced his mind to think.

How does the man in the moon get a haircut? Eclipse it.

What do you call two guys fighting over a prostitute? Tug of whore.

Mickey felt dazed. He saw the woman holding out a pen and paper. "We don't mind," she said. "Just your autograph will be fine."

"No, no," Mickey cried. "I have one now, a really good one." He felt immensely relieved. Whatever his mind had been doing to him, now it was back on track.

"What's big and yellow and lies on its back? A dead school bus."

The man was starting to get angry. "You've got a microphone hidden somewhere. You're trying to make us look like fools," he accused.

Mickey felt panicky. "Not at all," he said.

The man cut him short. "I've seen those programs. Thank you very much. We're not interested."

He seized his wife's arm and pulled her away. She took one last look over her shoulder. Mickey could read pity in her eyes.

Francisco had walked up. "How did that feel?" he said.

Mickey whirled on him in a rage. "Like crap. How do you think it felt? You did this to me, didn't you?"

Francisco opened his hands innocently. "I was just standing here."

Mickey wanted to blast him, but a wave of humiliation washed over him.

"I'm dying out here," he moaned. "This is a disaster."

His whole livelihood depended on his wits. Mickey closed his eyes, trying to steady himself. He knew exactly where to go to get his material.

Why did the cookie cry? Because his mother was a wafer so long.

How do you turn soup into gold? Add twenty-four carrots.

Oh my God. He felt physically sick.

"Pull yourself together," said Francisco.

Mickey glanced at him. Francisco didn't seem to be smirking or enjoying himself at Mickey's expense. Mickey took a couple of deep breaths until the feeling of being stuck inside a nightmare started to fade.

"What were you trying to teach me?" he said.

"Your ego only feels good when you're on. When you're clicking, you're alive. I wanted you to feel what it's like to be off."

"I don't want to be off," Mickey protested.

"I know. It's in the riddle." Francisco recited the last two lines again.

Protection is worth it, wouldn't you say?
Life is so empty when you don't get your way

"Ego has trapped you in a vicious circle," he explained. "It feeds you what you want, it keeps you moving from one desire to the next. But ego's game is like a leaky boat. You're only floating if you bail faster than the boat is sinking. So it goes from birth to death. Every day something new to chase after. In your case, the big allure is approval. The more you get, the more you want. Your idea of success is an unending flow of other people liking you."

"So?"

"So God forbid you should stop playing the ego's

79

game. Then what? You'd be terrified. In the quiet of your mind the gears would stop racing. A voice would rise from the darkness, and it would whisper in your ear, 'Nobody cares who you are. You're nothing.'"

"Maybe I am nothing," Mickey said mournfully. "You saw me back there."

"That's your truth right now," said Francisco. "But there's another truth. A better one."

"I'm listening."

"You're not nothing. In fact, you are everything. Literally. If you could stop being on all the time, your being would expand until it filled the universe. I know that sounds unbelievable. Are you up for another demonstration?"

Mickey nodded. They walked away from the pedestrian mall, and after a moment he said, "I told my ex I was starting to ask myself some questions."

"Did she believe you?"

"She seemed to think I still had lots of work to do."

"Don't expect anyone else to see what's going on inside you," Francisco warned. "The process is private, yet it happens the same way every time."

"Which is how?"

"When the pain of being the same becomes greater than the pain of being different, you change."

Francisco smiled, and for a fleeting instant Mickey

saw a face behind the stranger's: Larry. His father was still watching him. He wasn't in heaven yet. "They" were allowing him to connect with his son a little longer.

A moment later his glimpse of Larry was gone. Francisco was leading them back to the parking lot to the car. Mickey got behind the wheel.

"Where to now?" he said.

"We need a specialty store, one that carries women's clothes."

"Why didn't you say so before?" Mickey said. "There are women's stores on every corner."

Francisco shook his head. "Not that carry my size."

Mickey stopped asking questions. He turned the key in the ignition, and the big Cadillac roared to life.

5

M ICKEY HAD A VAGUE IDEA WHERE THEY COULD find a women's store catering to plus sizes, but he wasn't concentrating on that.

"Am I ever going to be on again?" he asked.

"We'll see," said Francisco. "Right now, you're taking a vacation from being Mickey Fellows."

"But that's how I earn my living," Mickey said, trying not to sound panicked.

"Yes, but he's just a role you've taken on. That's okay as long as you realize that you're playing a part. The real you isn't about roles."

The car had pulled up to a stoplight at a busy corner of Santa Monica Boulevard. Francisco pointed to half a dozen pedestrians waiting on the curb.

"Those people are as trapped in their roles as you are."

He nodded toward a teenager waiting for the light with a skateboard under his arm; he was standing next to a middle-aged man in a gray business suit.

"That kid thinks of himself as a rebel. In his eyes the

businessman is a sell-out. But if you look at it from the businessman's perspective, the kid is an irresponsible slacker who refuses to grow up. All of that is ego talk. The ego wants to feel superior. In reality, those two people are completely equal."

The Walk sign came on, and the pedestrians stepped off the curb, crossing in front of Mickey's car. "I want you to see them as equal," Francisco said. "It would change everything." He glanced over at Mickey. "You don't believe me."

"I just see a bunch of strangers. They probably have nothing in common."

"They're all souls," said Francisco. "To me, nothing else matters. Either you're a person wondering if you have a soul, or you're a soul who knows that being a person isn't real."

Mickey watched as the teenager jumped on his skateboard. He saw the dirty glances the kid was getting when he scooted too close to other people. The skater remained oblivious, lost in his own world. Before reaching the opposite side of the street, he veered off and shot down a lane of traffic. Horns blared at him before he swerved again and jumped the curb.

"Those cars aren't honking at a soul," Mickey pointed out.

"You say that because you buy into role-playing,

which makes your ego happy. It's got a lot invested in your self-image. Everything, in fact."

The light turned green; Mickey pulled the Escalade away. "I don't want to be the same as everyone else," he said. "You call that ego. I call it being myself. What's the big problem?"

For the moment Francisco didn't explain. He was paying attention to the strip malls and shops that lined the street.

"There's a convenience store. Pull in," he said.

"I thought you wanted a dress shop," Mickey said, but he turned in at the opening in the curb.

"This is more important for now," said Francisco, getting out of the car. He led Mickey to the door of the convenience store.

"What I want you to do is stand here," he said. "Open the door for anyone going in or out. Catch their attention, and when they notice you, hold your hand out for spare change."

"What?" Mickey couldn't think of anything he wanted to do less.

Francisco said, "You think you're going to be humiliated again. Try not to assume anything. I'll be back."

He turned and walked away, leaving Mickey to his ordeal. Customers were coming in and out of the store in a steady stream, so there was no time to debate the issue with himself. Mickey gave in. An older black woman was approaching the store. Mickey walked quickly to beat her to the door, then held it open. He smiled nervously. The woman nodded and gave him a quick look but nothing else. Her lack of reaction was a relief.

Half a minute later two kids who could have been in college were coming out of the store. When Mickey opened the door for them, they smirked and walked away without looking back. A deliveryman double-parked his van and ran into the store. Mickey watched as he bought a hot dog and a Coke, all the while keeping his eye on the van. He rushed back to it without giving Mickey a second glance.

Barely five minutes had passed, and Mickey was starting to calm down. He hadn't worked up the nerve to hold out his hand for change. Holding the door open was no more than an offhand courtesy, a little odd, but nothing like the annoyance of panhandling.

Are you going to do this thing or not? he asked himself.

A woman was approaching who looked better dressed than most, and she was talking into her cell phone. As he opened the door, Mickey held out his hand. She glanced down at it.

"Get a job."

The fact that she had interrupted her call to say this, and the snarl in her voice, made Mickey turn red. He almost ran away, but two more arrivals came up fast. Mickey opened the door and held out his hand. The couple burst out laughing and went past him. For a second he thought they had recognized him. That must be it—they had run into a famous comedian who was pulling some kind of stunt. But a minute later when they came out, the man handed him a quarter.

"You don't look like you need this," he said. "I hope it's not for drugs."

The man gave him a dead-serious look, and then the couple walked on. Suddenly Mickey caught on. Not a single person had recognized him, and therefore Francisco must be right. It was like taking a vacation from being Mickey Fellows. The thought sank in as he kept opening the door. People came and went. A few were hostile; most were indifferent. He was given another quarter, two dimes, and four pennies. Nobody knew who he was.

Mickey began to find this strangely liberating. After half an hour he stopped caring how the customers reacted. He'd turned into an impartial observer, a watcher of the passing parade. This was a novel experience. It amused him when the occasional person glanced down at his handmade Italian shoes, which cost a fortune, and looked puzzled by the sight of a panhandler in designer footwear. A grizzled old black man regarded him resentfully, as if Mickey had stolen his job. A woman who got out of a Lexus eyed him up and down as if he might be dating material.

"In the world but not of it."

Mickey turned around when he heard Francisco's voice.

"I think you're right," he said. "I'm a floater. Nobody cares who I am. Is that what you wanted me to feel?"

"Something like that."

Francisco was carrying a shopping bag, Mickey noticed before he turned back to the door and opened it for an old lady coming out with her pet dachshund.

"Nice dog," he said. "Spare change?"

The old lady scowled. "Creep."

Mickey grinned at Francisco. "Isn't that great? Even when they throw rocks, I don't feel it."

"Fun's over. Let's get some lunch."

When they got back to the car, Francisco threw his bag into the backseat. Once Mickey got in, he said, "How long did it take before you stopped feeling humiliated?"

"Not long. Fifteen minutes," Mickey said.

"Congratulations." Francisco seemed genuinely pleased. They were both in good spirits, in fact. For two days Mickey had felt manipulated. A stranger was foisting himself off as someone magical and mysterious.

Mickey had been in show business too long to believe in magic, and this led him to reject mystery as well. Yet unwittingly, he had let both creep back into his life.

They drove around as he thought about this.

"When you first walked up to me on the beach," he said, "you didn't think much of me, did you?"

"I saw potential," said Francisco.

"That doesn't answer my question."

"You were just a person to me," said Francisco.

"So in your scheme of things I was a nobody." Mickey surprised himself with a burst of laughter. "I've spent my whole life trying to be a somebody."

"Did you feel like a somebody back there?" Francisco asked.

"No. I was on vacation, just as you said. And I liked it. That's what I can't get over."

"You're starting to see through the tricks of your ego. It's deeply relaxing to get out from under the constant demands of 'I, me, and mine.' You breathe easier," said Francisco.

"So the big secret is to be a nobody all the time?" Mickey said.

"It's not that simple. Nobodies have egos, too. Theirs happen to be crushed, while yours is on the rampage."

Mickey could have been offended, but he grinned instead. "I'm lucky you're fixing me."

He had the feeling that this remark didn't sit well with Francisco, who went quiet and stared out the passenger window. But all he said was, "Tell me a joke."

"I can't," said Mickey. "You've done something to my brain."

"Try anyway."

Reluctantly Mickey went inside to the place where he found his material, a place that felt oddly empty now. A joke came to him, however.

An evil wizard captures a beautiful princess and imprisons her in his tower. She begs piteously to be released, and the wizard says, "I will let any knight try to save you, but on one condition."

He points to the filthy burlap his dog used as a bed. "You must make a dress from that burlap and wear it night and day."

The princess agrees. Every day a different knight in shining armor comes to her tower, but after one glance they all ride away.

The princess is baffled. "What's wrong with me?" she asks the wizard. "Am I not beautiful?"

"That's not it," the wizard says. "Knights won't rescue a damsel in this dress."

"No good," Mickey said. Why wasn't he more bothered? An hour ago the prospect of being off had caused acute anxiety. Now it was almost a relief.

"What's happening to me?" he asked.

"You are standing at the doorway," said Francisco. "Behind you is the world you know, a world that hides from fear and obeys the desires of the ego. In front of you is the unknown. The question is, will you step through the door?"

"Do you know the answer?" Mickey asked.

"Yes."

"Tell me."

"I can't. But I can let you peek over the threshold. Stop the car anywhere," said Francisco.

Mickey pulled over on a side street lined with bungalows and palm trees. If he was on a spiritual journey—and it seemed undeniable that he was—it certainly involved a lot of driving and parking.

Francisco turned the rearview mirror toward Mickey. "Look at yourself," he said. "I want you to see what's in the mirror. Don't assume you know."

"But I do know," said Mickey.

"No, there's someone you haven't met yet. He's on the other side of the threshold." Mickey looked at his reflection. Francisco went on. "See somebody who isn't funny, who isn't rich and famous. Forget that you know his name."

"It's not working," said Mickey.

"Concentrate on the eyes."

The rearview mirror was narrow enough so that if

Mickey leaned in close, all he could see was his eyes. He'd never given them a second thought. Women had told him they were large. Whenever he was performing, he felt that they lit up onstage.

They weren't lit up now. The eyes gazing back at him were flat. Like chips of gray-blue marble. Mickey squinted, trying to make them sparkle with amusement. Nothing changed. He widened them, trying to look surprised. He glanced out of the corners of his eyes, trying to look sly. It was uncanny, but whatever he did, nobody was at home. Behind his irises was empty space. Blankness.

Mickey sat back. "That's enough."

"What did you see?" asked Francisco.

"Nothing. Is there supposed to be a right answer here?" said Mickey, suddenly feeling nervous.

"Maybe 'nothing' *is* the right answer. It could be another name for the unknown. I think you caught a glimpse of a stranger. Don't back off that. He's the one you were meant to meet."

"Why? He didn't say anything. He didn't show me anything."

Mickey felt resentful. The morning had been going well. He felt good about what had happened at the convenience store, but glancing in the mirror had spoiled it somehow. If he had met the person he was supposed to meet, it had sure left him with a hollow feeling after-wards.

Without warning his mind clicked into gear.

"Hold on," he said. "There was this Indian doctor who had just come to America. He was invited to a fancy cocktail party with his wife, who didn't speak English. The host came up and said, 'Do you have children?'

"'Oh no,' the doctor replied. 'My wife here is unbear-able.' The host looked confused. The Indian doctor grew nervous. 'I mean to say, she is inconceivable.'

"Now the host was totally baffled. In frustration the Indian doctor cried, 'Don't you understand? My wife is impregnable!'"

Mickey laughed at his joke, and when he glanced over at Francisco, he was laughing, too.

"My vacation's over, isn't it?" he said. Francisco nod-ded. Mickey was on again. Should he be grateful for that? At that very moment he couldn't make up his mind.

WHEN FRANCISCO SAID they should have lunch, Mickey didn't imagine that he meant at the Bel-Air Hotel. But they were pulling up to it now, across expanses of expensive greenery and doormen in equally expensive cutaway coats.

"You're sure about this?" Mickey asked. A uniformed valet was approaching.

"Yes. Just let me do something first," Francisco said.

The valet opened the driver's door and handed Mickey a ticket. At a glance he recognized him. "Welcome back, Mr. Fellows," he murmured, in the gentle tones used to soothe a celebrity. Without warning, this was followed by a raised eyebrow. Mickey glanced over his shoulder.

Francisco had pulled the shopping bag from the backseat and opened it, extracting a shoe box. Now he was holding up a pair of red high heels. They were enormous.

"You're not going to wear those," said Mickey.

"Only the right one." Calmly, as if the valet wasn't gawking, Francisco took off the beach sandal he was wearing on his right foot and replaced it with a red high heel.

"Tight," he said. "But close enough." He put the other shoe back in the box.

Mickey was too flummoxed to speak. Francisco opened his door and got out. He took a step and almost fell over. "You're going to have to help me," he said.

Mickey reached into his pocket, found a twenty-dollar bill, and shoved it into the valet's hand. The valet wiped the astonishment off his face. "Just go," Mickey said.

When the car had been whisked away, he went up to Francisco. "You're not going to do this. You look ridiculous."

Francisco grabbed on to Mickey's arm and started tottering toward the front door. "What do you care?" he said. "I'm the one who has to manage a stiletto. You should try it sometime."

He was clearly enjoying himself. Mickey ducked his head, avoiding the looks they were getting from the two doormen ahead of them. Like the valet, they murmured, "Nice to see you again, Mr. Fellows."

Hobbling on his one high heel, Francisco made it to the dining room, a sumptuous retreat full of crystal and plush. "Table in the middle," he told the maitre d', who shot a baffled glance at Mickey.

Mickey nodded grimly. They were shown to a large table in full view of the whole room. The sight of a tall man with a spade beard wobbling on one red high heel was hard to ignore. There were titters.

Francisco winced as he sat down. "This really pinches." He took the shoe off and set it on an empty chair beside him. It glowed like a stop sign. The titters grew louder.

"They're laughing," he pointed out. "Maybe you should put this bit in your act."

"There's good laughing and there's bad laughing,"

Mickey growled. He waved away the menu offered by the waiter. "Just bring me a piece of fish. We're in a hurry." He noticed Francisco studying his menu, which was pages long. "Don't prolong this," he said sourly.

Francisco ignored him and ordered two courses with a glass of Chardonnay. "You love good laughing and hate bad laughing, is that it?" he said after the waiter was gone.

"Get to the point," Mickey snapped.

"Your ego tries to build you up. It makes you feel special and protected. But what's really happening? You wind up being incredibly insecure." He indicated the tables around the room. "Perfect strangers laugh at you, and suddenly the whole facade collapses. There was never any protection. You were never safe."

By the time the waiter returned with a plate of poached salmon, Mickey had lost his appetite. "You're right. I am insecure," he admitted. "But you scare me. If I listen to you, everything I've built up could collapse. Then what would I do?"

"There's nothing wrong with what you do," said Francisco. "You tell jokes. Jokes catch people off guard and make them laugh. That's not real happiness, but at least it provides a clue."

"What is real happiness?" asked Mickey.

"Being at one with your soul," Francisco said without hesitation.

"Okay, then what's a soul?"

"Everything that the ego is not."

Mickey shook his head. "How do you know all this?"

Francisco was amused. "You've been asking yourself that for a while." He leaned closer and lowered his voice to a conspiratorial whisper. "I'll tell you my secret. Are you ready? I'm not a person."

"What kind of secret is that?" Mickey asked.

"A very important one. When we walked into this restaurant I was playing the fool. People started laughing. To you it was the bad kind of laughing, because they were laughing at me. Just to be around me made you feel embarrassed. You became a fool by proximity."

"I can't help it."

"I know. You're a person who thinks he might have a soul. I'm a soul who knows he's playing the role of a person. Those people weren't laughing at me. They were laughing at my performance."

This explanation made sense to Mickey. "At the convenience store I was playing the part of a panhandler. I'm not really one. So after a while I could separate myself from it."

"See?" said Francisco.

Mickey's spirits had risen enough that he could actually eat. The food was delicious, and it gave him space to think. After a moment he said, "So you don't play any roles at all?"

"Not unless I choose to. And when I play a role, I know that the real me isn't performing. It's watching, a bit involved but essentially keeping to itself."

Mickey thought back to the people who had insulted him when he opened the door for them and held out his hand for spare change. One called him a creep, one told him to get a job. The barbs didn't sting, and now he knew why. He could be completely detached. Playing a part made him safe when he didn't identify with it.

"I think the process is working," he said. "But I have to be honest. I still don't know what the process is."

"I'll show you here and now," Francisco said. Sitting in front of him were two glasses, one filled with water and the other with wine. "I ordered white wine for a reason. Watch."

He picked up the two glasses and carefully poured one into the other, then back again, until wine and water were completely mixed. "You can't tell the two apart now," he said. "So what if I wanted to separate them again? How can I get water back into one glass and wine into the other?"

Mickey shook his head. "You can't."

"Right. But the process can. Your soul and your ego are as invisibly mixed as white wine and water. That's why people are so confused. They wander through life searching for the soul when it's right there all the time. They talk about losing their soul when that's totally impossible. They believe their soul will go to Heaven after they die, but the soul is everywhere already.

"In other words, the soul is a mystery. It can't be lost or found. It is neither here nor there. It belongs to you and yet it belongs to God. Without a process, no one would ever get to the bottom of it."

These words made a deep impression on Mickey. Not for the first time he wanted to grab Francisco's arm and say, "Who are you?" Seeing the look of wonder on his face, Francisco grinned. "Don't get freaked out. I'm not the Second Coming, or whatever you think I am."

They finished their food in silence. Walking out of the hotel back to the valet stand, Mickey felt different. There was no precise term for what was happening to him. Francisco picked up on it.

"You're searching for a label," he said. "Don't. The process can't be named. It's invisible and yet all-powerful. It alters everything you say and do, yet nothing you say and do is part of it."

At that moment, what he was hearing matched Mickey's ineffable feeling. He was floating inside a mystery. But once they had retrieved his car and were driving down Sunset toward the shore, Mickey lost his sense of wonder. It was like gossamer, too ethereal to hold on to. Francisco picked up on this, too.

"You can't own the process," he said. "You can't cling to it, any more than you could hold on to the smell of the ocean. The process happens entirely in the present. It's here one second and gone the next. Anyway, I have a joke for you.

"A little girl is taken to a restaurant by her parents. The waiter stands by while they read the menu. The little girl says, 'I want a hamburger.'

"The mother looks over at the father. 'How does a Greek salad sound?'

"'Fine,' he replies.

"'We'll have three Greek salads,' the mother tells the waiter.

"Turning to the kitchen, the waiter shouts, 'Two Greek salads and a hamburger.'

"'Look, Mommy,' the little girl exclaims. 'He thinks I'm real!'"

After a moment, Mickey said, "So you think I'm real?"

"Yes, even if you don't."

The thought made Mickey feel better. The sun was warm on his face. The sky was cloudless and bright. He had enjoyed laughing at Francisco's joke, and for a fleeting instant it seemed as if everything around him was laughing, too.

6

ICKEY'S ELATION DIDN'T COMPLETELY FADE AS they drove along. He felt light-headed and had to pay attention to the road. Whenever Sunset Boulevard took a big curve, it felt like the car was turning into a glider. As if it might swoop into the air and catch the next breeze.

"This is unreal," Mickey murmured softly.

"It's more unreal not to feel this way," said Francisco. "This is your bliss. Soak it up."

Mickey looked out the window at the stream of cars racing in both directions and the handsome stucco houses drifting by. He had heard of out-of-body experiences. He wondered if this was one. Neither man spoke, and it seemed as if the ribbon of road would unfold forever. Sunset Boulevard dipped toward the ocean. The western sun came straight into Mickey's eyes, and the glare made him blink.

"I'm coming back down. I can feel it," he said.

Francisco glanced over at him. "Don't worry. Glide a little longer. We're in no hurry to make a landing."

Mickey kept having the sensation that he wasn't driving but merely watching the road unfold. Gradually, though, he returned to what he thought of as his senses.

"Why is all this happening to me?" he asked, turning to Francisco. "I really need to know."

"I'm only playing my part," Francisco said. "It's like a game of tag. I found you just the way somebody once found me."

This was the first time that he had made any reference to his personal life. Mickey pounced on it. "Someone walked up to you on a beach?"

"No, at work. I was a builder. A stranger showed up on-site. I got annoyed, but pretty soon that didn't matter." Francisco saw the curiosity in Mickey's eyes. "Nothing from before much matters. You'll see."

An hour earlier it would have scared Mickey to hear this. Some part of him had accepted the process, but another part had kept alive the belief that he could go back to normal anytime he wanted. But normal was shifting, and he wasn't scared now. "Does the process last your whole life?" he asked.

"Yes, but it keeps changing. When I started out, I felt as much fear as you did. I resisted every bit as much, even though I didn't have your inflated ego. No offense. And don't worry. When the process is over, that will be gone, too."

The prospect suddenly seemed like the best news Mickey had ever heard.

"I want to go for it," he said. "Can we speed things up?"

Francisco was amused. "You might singe your eyebrows or melt your wings. Be careful."

"Were you careful?"

Francisco shook his head. "No. I went off course. Just for a while. My guide was worried."

Now that they had reached the beach, Mickey expected to turn south, the direction of home. Francisco pointed to a supermart on the corner. "Just pull in there."

Mickey pulled off the road and parked. "Who was your guide?" he asked.

"His name was Martin. He was a one-man mystery school. What he knew about life. . ." Francisco's voice trailed off.

He turned to Mickey. "None of this is magical. Guides aren't wizards. They don't float down from another world," he said. "They are just striking a match in the darkness, or offering a jump start. Anyway, you and I still have some unfinished business."

Fishing inside his shirt pocket, Francisco handed Mickey a folded piece of paper. He said, "Bliss comes and goes unless you nail it down. That's the next step." He watched as Mickey opened up and read the latest riddle.

One day you love me, the next day you hate
But you never resist the hook and the bait
You cry for escape, but what do I care?
The net that I cast is a permanent snare

Mickey furrowed his brow. "I don't get it. This is about cravings or something."

"Close." Francisco took back the riddle and wrote a word on the back: "Addiction."

Mickey shook his head. "I'm not addicted. I've never even checked into rehab for the publicity."

"This isn't about drugs, or sex, or alcohol. That blissful feeling you just experienced? It goes away because you keep going back to your old self. That's the worst addiction. As long as you crave the old self, you can never fully contact the unknown."

"So I'm addicted to myself?"

"You're addicted to your *old* self. Everyone is." Francisco looked in the direction of a nearby bus stop. "To be continued. I have to go."

Mickey didn't want to be left with nothing but a few frustrating clues. "Wait," he said. "Aren't you going to tell me how to break out of this?"

Francisco was already out of the car. "It's time you start fending for yourself."

"What does that mean?" Mickey asked sullenly.

Francisco leaned back into the open passenger-side window. "Cheer up. You're on the right track." Looking over his shoulder, he saw a city bus easing toward the curb. He said, "Send me off with half a laugh. A quick one, before that bus goes away."

"You know the difference between a bar and a pharmacy?" said Mickey. "Smaller inventory."

"That's half a laugh. Now go home and look in the mirror again. You'll meet someone who has the answers you want."

Francisco ran for the bus, which had let out its last passenger. He jumped on, and after the doors swung shut behind him Mickey could see Francisco making his way down the center aisle looking for a seat. How many passengers, he thought, had any idea who was among them?

MICKEY HAD THOUGHT that he would go look in the mirror, but once he got home he put it off. He was feeling flat. Payback had been lonely, cooped up all day. She jumped on him with hysterical yaps. Mickey fed her, then scrounged up some leftover sushi and a beer from the fridge. His voice mail contained seven new messages.

He wasn't in the mood to answer any of them except his agent's.

"What's been going on?" Alicia said when he got hold of her.

"Do you think I'm addicted?"

"What?"

Mickey repeated the question.

"Yeah, you're addicted," Alicia said. "To money, approval, and chocolate, just like the rest of us. Unless you mean the hard stuff."

"Anything else?"

"Let me see. Single-malt Scotch, golf, and being funny. Should I go on?"

"I didn't know you thought I was funny," said Mickey.

"Off and on. What's with you? You sound different."

I got a gig in a mystery school. A complete stranger tapped me as a freshman. Next week he thinks I'll be ready to fly.

Mickey didn't hint at what he was thinking. "I've been relaxing. Working on some one-liners," he said, and rattled off a couple.

"A clear conscience is the first sign that you're losing your memory.

"A flashlight is a device for finding dead batteries in the dark."

Idly munching on the sushi, Mickey opened a sliding

glass door and carried the cell phone out on the deck. He had the urge to really make Alicia laugh. "Forget those. Here's a good joke," he said.

"A 911 operator gets a call from a man who sounds frantic. 'I'm on a hunting trip, and I accidentally shot my friend.'

"The 911 operator says, 'The first thing we have to do is make sure if he's dead.'

"She hears a loud bang, then the guy comes back on. 'Okay,' he says. 'He's dead. Now what?'"

Alicia gave a muffled groan that could have bespoken amusement. She told Mickey to keep working, and hung up. By then Mickey no longer wanted to watch the sunset. He was slipping back into his old self. Francisco told him this was his addiction, and now Alicia had more or less sealed the case. He got up and shooed Payback back into the house, shutting the sliding glass door behind them.

Look in the mirror again. You'll meet someone who has the answer.

The moment had come. Mickey found a mirror in the guest bathroom off the front entry. He leaned against the vanity and stared at himself. Narrowing his eyes, he concentrated, waiting for something to happen.

Nothing happened.

Maybe it wasn't about concentrating. Mickey smiled at

his reflection. "How's it going? I'm great, too. Thanks for asking." The eyes staring back at him weren't flat and empty the way they had been in the car. That part was good. He relaxed and gazed into his eyes again. A few minutes passed.

He got bored.

But if he gave up now, he'd have nothing to show for his effort. Mickey leaned closer to his reflection. He pretended that he was an optometrist peering into his eyes with a scope, right into the pupil. . . .

His pupils grew larger. Then one eye, the right, kept on dilating, until Mickey thought his iris would disappear. Freakish as this was, he kept calm. Only then did he realize that his pupil wasn't expanding—he was being drawn into its growing point of darkness. As it began to envelop him, Mickey remembered a TV image from his childhood, Zorro flourishing his black cape in the air. The cape swept over Mickey like nightfall, and then everything faded to black.

"Hello?" he called. His voice echoed as if in an empty auditorium.

"Hello?"

In answer, a tiny point of light appeared in the distance. There was nowhere else to go, so Mickey headed toward it. When he got closer he saw what it was. A flashlight. The man holding it was sitting on a stool.

"Look out, kiddo," the man said. "The ice is slippery and not all that thick."

It was Larry.

Mickey rushed toward him, hearing the ice creak beneath his feet.

"What are you doing?" he said, although he knew. A man sitting on a stool staring into a hole in the ice must be ice fishing. It had been Larry's favorite winter pastime when Mickey was a boy. He remembered his father dragging him out of his warm bed and driving their old Ford pickup to a godforsaken lake in Wisconsin.

"I've become a fisher of men," said Larry, tugging on his line.

"Really?" Mickey said.

"I caught you, didn't I?"

Larry sounded so much like Larry that it was all Mickey could do not to reach out and touch him, to make sure he was real. But his instincts told him not to try.

His father waved his flashlight in the dark. The beam landed on a second stool on the other side of the hole. Mickey sat down.

"I don't think it's legal to use a flashlight," he said.

"Damn souls won't bite unless you do," said Larry. He grinned. "Same as pike."

Maybe because this was the second time, Mickey wasn't at all surprised to see Larry. He felt relaxed but cold, happy to be spending time with his dad, but not really loving the fishing. It wasn't all that different from when he was ten.

"Everything changes and nothing changes, eh, kiddo?" said Larry.

"Are you still in limbo?"

Larry shrugged. "It's okay. I get out once I stop worrying about you."

This news unsettled Mickey. "You can stop worrying," he said. "Go where you need to go."

"Settle down. I'm not in prison. Didn't you come to ask me something?" said Larry.

"I came to ask somebody something," Mickey said uncertainly.

"Ask your old man." Larry looked over at his son and read the expression on his face. "We never talked much. I regret that," he said.

"I could have tried harder, too," said Mickey.

Larry sighed. "Remember the day you got cut from the school baseball team? You were pretty good for your size, but they wanted bigger players for varsity. You had the skill but not the beef. You were really broken up."

"That was a long time ago."

"When you do wrong, it stays in the present, no matter how much time passes."

"What did I do wrong?" said Mickey.

"Not you, me." Larry fiddled around with his fishing line, thinking something over. "You wanted me to comfort you, but I didn't know how. You ran up to me the way you used to when you were eight or nine, and you tried to hug me. All I could think of was, the kid's too old for this. I pushed you away. Remember that?"

"You said, 'If you want a hug, go hug your mother,'" said Mickey. "It wasn't a big deal."

"Yes, it was." Larry paused. "I cut the cord between us. The worst of it was, I knew it. I could feel that you and I were never going to be the same. I loved you, damn it, and I pushed you away. For what?"

The sorrow in his father's voice put a lump in Mickey's throat. "Sons go away, Dad."

"You didn't come back," said Larry. "You do have to send a son away. But you do it when you both know it's right, and you do it in such a way that he can come back again."

What could Mickey say? It scared him to think that Larry was in limbo because he had so much guilt. Before Mickey could open his mouth, his father's gloom lifted as suddenly as it had come over him.

"Not to worry. I had to tell you, but it's gone now." Larry looked upward and scanned the darkness. "You can't see them, but they really do help. God's people, I mean." He coughed and his body gave a small shiver. "Where was I? Oh, the question you wanted to ask."

Mickey hadn't recovered yet from his father's admission. Larry had been old-fashioned when he was alive. He didn't show emotion. When he hugged you, it was a man hug, where you put one arm around the other man's shoulder and give a few reluctant pats.

"Give me a minute," Mickey said.

"Okay. You want to hear God's favorite joke?" Larry asked.

"Sure."

Larry sat up and looked Mickey in the eyes. "Sin," he said. He started to chuckle, but nothing else followed.

"That's the joke?" said Mickey.

"Absolutely. Whenever God hears that people believe in sin, it cracks him up."

"And you can hear him laughing," said Mickey.

"To beat the band," said Larry. Then he caught himself. "I have way too much leisure time these days." He pulled his trotline out of the water and started to wrap it up around his gloved hand. Mickey noticed that the line had no hooks or bait. "Doesn't matter," said Larry. "Souls aren't biting anyway."

He gathered his tackle and stood up. "So it's now or

never, kiddo. Ask me your question. I gotta go pretty soon."

His tone was lighter now, but Mickey knew that his father wanted to make amends. Regret hung over him like mist rising from the ice. Mickey didn't expect any kind of answer, but he asked anyway.

"I'm stuck on myself, on my way of doing things," he said. "I don't love the way I am, but I'm addicted to it, and I don't know how to stop."

"That's easy," Larry said, looking relieved. "I thought you were going to ask me how to get your wife back. No one can help you there."

"Help me here," Mickey implored.

"Okay. Are you listening?" Larry cleared his throat. "You keep on doing what never worked in the first place. Don't."

"What?"

"Addictions are artificial substitutes. You're stuck on things that never bring you what you really want. You can't have real roses, so you buy plastic ones. You can't think sweet thoughts, so you gobble down sugar. You can't figure out how to be happy, so you make other people laugh."

"When will I stop doing that?"

"Good question."

Larry seemed increasingly restless. From time to time he glanced over his shoulder into the surrounding night.

"I'm coming, I'm coming," he said impatiently.

He turned back to Mickey. "They give me limited access. I guess I told you that the first time. What can you do?" He gave a shrug and began to walk away, his heavy rubber boots causing the ice to groan.

Mickey called after him. "Why didn't you come through the TV? I still believe in television, just like you said."

Larry didn't look back. "Don't worry. You believe in darkness, too."

And then he disappeared.

MICKEY CAME BACK without knowing how. One minute he was on the ice in the darkness, and the next minute he was standing in front of the mirror again. It was a mystery, but it had to wait in line to be solved. Mysteries had been piling up around him pretty thick recently.

He went back into the kitchen where he'd left the last of his sushi and beer. Mickey felt calm. The house seemed very quiet around him. Payback stared up from her terry-cloth bed by the stove, whined, and wagged her tail. Mickey walked over. He whispered in her ear. "Did you

hear about the paranoid dyslexic? He was sure he was following somebody."

Payback yapped and nipped at his nose.

"That's okay. Bite all you want. In dog years I'm
already dead."

Mickey didn't know why he was in such good humor.
He sat down at the kitchen counter sipping his beer, not
thinking about anything. But Larry's words returned on
their own.

You keep on doing what never worked in the first place.

Okay. Now what?

Francisco had told him it was time to fend for himself. Mickey wanted to. He had been yearning for a different life for a long time. It had taken Larry's death to
make him realize it. But how could he give up his addiction?

Mickey tossed the empty beer can into the trash and
picked up Payback.

"Come on, girl. You and me."

It was barely ten o'clock when he and the dog got
settled in bed. Mickey grabbed the remote and channel
surfed. What caught his eye was a familiar sight. A helicopter hovered over the 405 Freeway. Down below, the
cops were in pursuit of a stolen SUV. Mickey turned up
the sound.

"What began as a high-speed chase several hours ago

has turned into a grueling slow-motion endurance test," the announcer said over the helicopter shot. "The suspect, now identified as Alberto Rodriguez, was originally fleeing to the Mexican border. Now it seems that he is leading police in circles."

From the overhead shot, it looked like the SUV was barely crawling down the road, tailed by five cop cars. Mickey had seen such images before. But this time he imagined himself being the driver. What was he thinking? The end of the chase was inevitable. He would run out of gas, the car would stall, and the police would close in.

The driver was just continuing to do what hadn't worked in the first place.

Mickey hit the mute button and phoned his mother. It was midnight in Chicago, but he knew she liked to stay up late.

"Hello?"

"Mom, it's me."

His mother sounded surprised. They had talked right after Larry's death. She hadn't come to the funeral. Her second husband didn't want her to, and anyway, she hadn't been on speaking terms with Larry for the last twenty years.

"Is something wrong?" she said.

"No, Mom, everything's fine. I wanted to ask you something. Why did you and Larry fight so much?"

"You want to ask me that now? It was so long ago. I can't remember."

"But you remember fighting?"

"God, yes. It was awful. We were both scrappers." Her tone became abrupt. "Do we really need to go into it right this minute?"

Mickey knew his mother was uncomfortable, but he couldn't get the image of the slow-motion highway chase out of his mind.

"Didn't you see where it was going?" he said. "People who keep on fighting end up getting a divorce."

"I'm sorry, honey."

"That's not what I mean. I can't figure out why you didn't try something different."

"I don't see what you're getting at."

"Neither of you was going to win, but you kept hacking away at each other."

"Honey, I don't want to throw stones, but you and Dolores got a divorce, too. You had fights. Did you ever stop thinking you'd win?"

Mickey wanted to say, *That's different. You were my parents. I was a kid when I got married. I couldn't handle it.*

Instead he said, "You're right. I shouldn't have

called. Go to bed, Mom." He mumbled an apology and hung up.

On the television the slow-mo car chase was still unfolding. The driver refused to quit. He'd eventually have to stop; it was inevitable. But his brain wouldn't accept the inevitable.

"Poor bastard," Mickey muttered.

He left the picture on mute as he rolled over in bed. TV helped him get to sleep. The morning news would tell him how it had all turned out.

7

THE FIRST RAY OF SUN STRUCK MICKEY'S SLEEP-
ing face, creating a rosy glow behind his eyelids. He
sat up and looked around, yawning. He felt content,
which surprised him; everything had been moving so
fast. Now the air felt cool and still. He saw that the TV
was still on mute, but he had no interest in the flickering
images playing across the screen.

A light tap at the sliding glass door broke the still-
ness.

"Come out here. I have something to show you."

It was Francisco. Mickey pulled on a shirt and pants
and opened the door to the deck.

"What do you think?" Francisco asked.

He didn't have to explain what he meant. Massive
thunderheads had built up over the ocean. Mickey had
never seen anything quite like it.

"Glorious," he murmured. It wasn't a word he'd ever
used before.

"Turn around," said Francisco.

Mickey did, and there were thunderheads behind them, too. As his gaze traveled around the sky, the same colossal cloud formations were everywhere.

"Strange, wouldn't you say?" said Francisco.

Mickey was still groggy with sleep, but suddenly he knew what Francisco meant. The only spot that was sunny was where they stood. He walked to the railing of the deck and looked down. The darkness created by the clouds came right up to his house and stopped. He and Francisco were in an island of light.

"Did you do this?" Mickey asked.

"Have you ever heard of a person who could control the weather?"

Mickey shook his head. "No."

"Then if I did this, I must not be a person." Francisco laughed at Mickey's reaction. "Here," he said, holding out his hand.

"What is it?"

"A graduation present."

Francisco opened his hand to reveal three small objects: a gold ring, a gold nugget, and a gold signet seal. They had been rubbed to a high polish and gleamed in the sunlight. Mickey felt uneasy. The three objects seemed like another riddle he couldn't unravel. Francisco read his mind.

"They contain the secret of happiness," he said. "I couldn't think of anything better."

"Are you going to tell me the secret?"

"You'll know. Go ahead, take them."

Mickey did, reluctantly. "What if I'm not ready to graduate? It seems awfully soon."

"No one's forcing you," said Francisco. "You can decide if you're ready."

The two began walking down the beach. Francisco's eyes searched the horizon, but Mickey saw nothing out at sea, not even the usual pleasure boats and cavorting sea lions. They approached a small pile of flotsam that high tide had left behind. Francisco stooped and pulled a damp crooked stick from the tangled seaweed.

"Just what we need," he said.

With the tip of the stick he drew a line in the sand. "We've come to your last lesson. The big one."

"All right," said Mickey uncertainly.

Francisco pointed to either side of the line he had drawn. "Over here is you and your world. Over here is God and God's world. Ever since you were born, you haven't crossed the boundary that separates them. Now you can."

"Wouldn't I have to die?"

Francisco shook his head. "God's world opens when you know the difference between illusion and reality. As I told you before, you have bought into the illusion that you are a person searching for his soul. The reality is that you are a soul playing the role of a person. Once you truly get that, you won't be a prisoner anymore. You'll be free."

Mickey hesitated. "Are you in God's world right now?"

"Yes."

"What's it like, exactly? I really want to know."

"There's nothing to fear, nothing to lose, nothing to be attached to. You won't recognize your old self anymore. You will get to be who you really are. "

"Excuse me, but that sounds a lot like dying." Mickey meant this as a halfhearted joke. But Francisco suddenly kicked the sand, and the line was gone.

"What's wrong?" Mickey said.

Francisco stared hard at him. "I wonder if you realize what I'm offering you. If you did, you would want it with every fiber of your being. Either that or you'd run away screaming, scared out of your skull."

"Sorry."

Francisco observed that Mickey's chagrin was genuine, but made no comment. "It's early. Let's see what the day brings," he said casually.

They continued down the beach. The opening in the cloud bank moved with them. Mickey didn't feel contented anymore.

"You're asking for a huge change. Maybe it's too much for me," he said. "I feel helpless."

"Not helpless enough," said Francisco.

"What does that mean?"

"You still think you're in control. It comes back to ego. The ego never gives up trying to be in control. So it keeps doing more and more of what didn't work in the first place."

"That's exactly what Larry told me. I saw him again," said Mickey.

"He was right. You won't change until your ego gives up. And it will only give up when you feel totally helpless. Then its game comes to an end. You face the unknown. It's scary and dark. But that's where you have to go."

Mickey wanted more of an explanation, but Francisco's mind was already elsewhere. "See that guy over there?" he asked.

Under a nearby lifeguard tower, Mickey could see a greenish pile of rags. It took a moment before he made out that it was a man curled up in a filthy army surplus coat.

"Yeah, I see him."

"How much money do you have on you?" said Francisco.

Mickey always kept quite a bit. He opened his wallet

and pulled out a wad of hundreds. "Okay," said Francisco. "Take out two hundred dollars. Go over there and give it to him. Let's see what happens. I'll hold on to the rest."

Mickey did as he was told. After a moment he came back.

"Well?" Francisco said.

"He was blown away. He was sleeping one off, so at first he thought I was going to bust him. When I put the money in his hands, he couldn't believe it. He started to cry."

They could both see the man. He had come out from under the lifeguard tower. His grizzled face wore a jubilant look, and he started waving madly at Mickey. Mickey waved back.

"That felt pretty good," he said, watching the man walk away. Every few seconds he'd look back and wave again.

Mickey looked down. Francisco was crouched in the sand. He had crumpled the rest of the hundreds into a small pile and set them on fire.

"What are you doing?" Mickey cried. He kicked at the little mound of flames, but Francisco blocked his foot.

"Just watch," he said.

"What do you mean, watch? That's a thousand bucks, maybe more!" Mickey exclaimed.

When there was no chance of rescuing the money, Francisco said, "How do you feel now?"

"Lousy. What's your point?" said Mickey sourly.

"I wanted you to see how predictable you are. When you gave your money away, you felt good. When you lost your money, you felt bad. That's all the ego has to offer: feeling good and feeling bad. You're like a rat in a lab experiment."

"Expensive experiment," said Mickey without enthusiasm.

"Have I made my point?"

"Tell me again." Mickey wasn't over the shock of seeing a pile of money reduced to ashes.

"You're too resentful right this minute," said Francisco. "You'll laugh once you see the truth. How about a laugh right now? Do you have a joke for me?"

Mickey knew this was a flimsy ploy, but he needed a diversion right now.

"A man is walking on the beach," he said. "And he finds a brass lamp buried in the sand. He rubs it, and out jumps a genie. 'You've set me free,' says the genie. 'Instead of granting you three wishes, I'll only grant you one, but it can be the biggest wish in the world.'

"The man thinks for a minute. 'I've never been to Hawaii. Build me a bridge so I can go there anytime I want.'

"'Are you crazy?' cries the genie. 'That's half the Pacific Ocean. Nobody can build a bridge that far. Make another wish.'

"The man thinks again. 'Okay, I want to know what women are really thinking.'

"'How wide do you want the bridge, one lane or two?' says the genie."

Mickey was relieved when Francisco laughed. The tension between them was broken, and they sat down together on the sand by the water's edge. After a minute a seagull circled overhead, searching for scraps. It piped shrilly and flew away disappointed.

"Why is that bird free and human beings aren't?" asked Francisco.

"It doesn't know any better?" Mickey guessed.

"Right, and it doesn't need to know better. It was born in God's world and has no reason to leave. So why do we? How did we come to believe that we must live on one side of the line while God lives on the other? When you think about it, it makes no sense. I don't care what religion someone believes in. And it wouldn't matter if God turns out to be he, she, or it. At the very least, God must be everywhere. Without that, God isn't God."

"So how do I get to everywhere?" Mickey asked.

Francisco smiled, but the next moment he became thoughtful. "I wanted to find God in the worst way when I was young," he said. "Wherever he was, somehow I wasn't. I struggled. I screamed, I cried. After I met my guide, he showed me something."

Francisco jumped to his feet. He tugged Mickey's arm, pulling him to the shore, and then knee-deep into the water. The cold sand sucked at their feet.

He asked, "How can you seek God if he's already here? It's like us standing in the ocean and crying out, 'I want to get wet.' You want to get over the line to God. It turns out he was always there." Francisco's eyes began to gleam. "Grace comes to those who stop struggling. When it really sinks in that there's nothing you can do to find God, he suddenly appears. That's the deepest mystery, the only one that counts."

MICKEY'S GRADUATION DAY wasn't spent entirely at the beach. Francisco declared that he was hungry and insisted on going to a specific place downtown. He wouldn't say why, but Mickey assumed he had a reason.

On the way, Francisco said, "You asked a brilliant question back there."

"I did?" said Mickey.

"Yes. You said, 'How do I get everywhere?' You and I are going to answer that. But if God is everywhere, the path to get there can't be a straight line. I'll show you what I mean."

Since Francisco had nothing more to say for the rest of the ride downtown, Mickey had time to consider his remarkable guide. Francisco's confidence was totally natural, yet as often as Mickey had observed it, he was still amazed. He wondered if it came with being free.

When downtown was in sight, Francisco came back to life. "We'll grab a bite, and then we're going back to where all the trouble began. The place where the connection was broken. Where human beings lost their innocence. Where God's love was lost, turning to hate, or at best indifference."

"You're talking about the Garden of Eden," said Mickey.

"Right. We need to go there. But not on an empty stomach."

They parked in a lot, and Francisco found the place where he wanted to eat, a Greek diner full of good smells—moussaka, lamb souvlaki revolving on a spit, white wine aged with pine resin. The food was earthy, like the short Greek couple that worked behind the counter. Mickey knew it was futile to try to hurry Francisco to the Garden of Eden, but at least Mickey could do his thing.

"Nobody tells Adam and Eve jokes anymore," he said. "I learned a lot of them as a kid.

"Why did God create Adam first? So he could have a chance to say something. That wouldn't be funny anymore. Maybe that's why those jokes went away. They were either blue or they put women down. Here's one that worked the last time I used it.

"God comes to Adam and says, 'I've got good news for you and bad news. Which one do you want to hear first?'

"'The good news,' says Adam.

"'Okay. I've given you a brain and a penis.'

"Adam says, 'That *is* good news. What's the bad news?'

"'I only gave you enough blood to run one at a time.'"

Even while he was talking, another part of Mickey's mind was watching Francisco closely. This might be the last time he would ever see his guide. Was it possible that he had learned enough from him? Would he never know Francisco's last name, or where he lived?

"I won't keep you in suspense," said Francisco, finishing the last of his gyro sandwich. He nodded at the building across the street. "That's where we're going."

"The county courthouse?"

"Specifically, divorce court," said Francisco. "It's as close to Eden as we can get. Both places begin with love and togetherness and end with anger and separation. I want to remind you how that feels."

The walk over to the courthouse was a short one. The interior halls were musty and dark. The second floor, where divorces were settled, felt sorrowful. Mickey saw people in pairs collecting around the doors before going into the courtrooms. The ones that looked like couples were actually lawyers and wives.

"They all look miserable," said Mickey, who had been there. "Why do we need to see this?"

"We don't," said Francisco. "The Garden of Eden may be a myth, but what does it stand for? A bad divorce between human beings and God. Now, what happens in a divorce? Both sides come out of it thinking they are right. When you're still married, there's room for give and take. You fight, and then you make up. In your heart of hearts you may still think you're right, but the two of you have to live together, and that means compromise.

"After the divorce it all changes. Your ex becomes totally wrong, and you are totally right. Those positions get frozen in place. Nobody budges, at least not for a long time."

Mickey said, "Who won the divorce from God?"

"It looked like he did. Human beings lost their innocence. They felt sinful. They figured that since they got thrown out of Paradise, there had to be a reason."

"Wasn't there?"

Francisco shook his head. "The divorce never took place. You asked me how to get to everywhere. You'll never get there if you think that you did something so bad that God decided to become your ex."

Francisco turned on his heels and headed for the elevators. Mickey trailed behind. "You sound pretty cynical," he said. "I don't expect that from you."

"I'm only being realistic. Love and togetherness does turn into anger and separation. Stand in these hallways and you'll see it a hundred times a day. Whether they know it or not, all those couples are reenacting an ancient drama."

Francisco punched the elevator button and waited. "I'd be cynical if I thought nothing could be done about it. But something can."

A few minutes later they were walking outside in the sunshine. Mickey had been considering his divorce from Dolores. It wasn't an accident that he had called her when he was upset. He was in the habit of intruding on her life, no matter how often she told him not to. At some level he knew why. He couldn't believe he had lost her. His mind wouldn't allow him to accept it.

"You still want to win," said Francisco.

Mickey was startled. "What?"

"You were thinking about your marriage. You want Dolores back because it would make you a winner. Divorce puts you in the loser's camp."

"That's kind of brutal," Mickey complained.

"Not if you look at it another way. You are in the grip of a wish that love could last forever. You don't want to believe it can turn to hatred. The same goes for the whole human race. Despite centuries of preaching about sin and the Fall of Man, people remember Paradise. They collect in churches to convince themselves that the divorce from God never took place."

"You just told me it didn't," said Mickey.

"It did if you believe it did. That's the power of illusion."

The palm trees circling the courthouse were old giants, and Mickey couldn't help imagining them as the same trees that provided shade in the Garden of Eden. A holdover from Sunday-school days and the Bible pictures shown to kids, perhaps.

"Divorce from God is a powerful illusion," said Francisco. "But since it isn't real, the way back is much simpler than it looks. What would it take for you to get back with your wife?" He didn't wait for Mickey to reply. "Something got between you, so that something needs to be removed."

"What is it?"

"You resisted each other. The give-and-take disappeared. By the end, one of you had to be right and the other wrong. See the point? To win her back, reverse the situation. Let *her* be right."

"I wish I could," said Mickey, shaking his head.

"You can," said Francisco. "If not with her, then with God. He is right and always has been, because in reality God is only love. He wants the best for you and nothing for himself. The slightest move on your part will be met with open arms."

Mickey took a deep breath. "Show me what to do, and I'll do it," he said.

"Deal," said Francisco. He gave Mickey an approving nod and began to walk away.

"What's going on?" Mickey exclaimed.

Francisco looked over his shoulder. "You just graduated. You made the right choice. Congratulations."

"You mean it ends here?" said Mickey in dismay.

"Yes. And it begins here. That's how these things work."

Francisco kept walking and Mickey felt a tremendous urge to run after him. Then he had second thoughts. Every time Francisco had gone away, he had eventually come back. Mickey only had to be patient. Meanwhile, Mickey had a lot to absorb. This day had been the most intense since they had met. Once Mickey was ready, his guide would reappear.

These thoughts were reassuring. They were also totally wrong. But Mickey wouldn't discover that for quite a while.

DAYS TURNED INTO weeks, and weeks into months. Mickey spent his private time doing strange things. He kept the television on night and day, just in case Larry had something to tell him. He spent an inordinate amount of time looking at himself in the mirror. His walks down the beach with Payback included at least one moment when Mickey thought he spotted a tall man with a goatee coming toward him in the distance.

Nobody knew about these odd behaviors. To the outside world he was the same old Mickey Fellows. Once he got back into the swing of things, Alicia found him more gigs than he could handle, plus a dozen movie scripts a week to consider. They gathered dust in a pile by his bed, untouched and unread.

Alicia was the one who came closest to sniffing him out. "You're different," she said one day on the phone.

"Different how?" said Mickey.

"I'm not sure. Like you were abducted by aliens, but they decided to be nice."

As far as the rest of the world was concerned, Mickey wasn't different at all. Hadn't Francisco told him that nobody would notice?

Of all the things his guide had shown him, a single image stuck in Mickey's mind: a line drawn in the sand. He began to think that Francisco must have crossed it forever. In any case, after three months Mickey woke up one morning with the realization that he was truly alone.

If God listens in on our thoughts, this must have been the one he was waiting for.

At first nothing seemed out of the ordinary. Mickey hopped out of his car in the Palisades to grab some Chinese takeout. The place was crazy busy, and someone walking out bumped into Mickey coming in. The guy was on his cell. He looked up and mumbled, "Sorry, bud," then kept on walking.

Mickey stared at him. "Arnie?" he called.

The man turned around, his ear still glued to his phone. "Yeah? Do I know you?"

"Maybe not. My mistake."

The guy nodded and went to his car. Mickey stood

there, wondering. He knew Arnie. They had started out in the same clubs. They'd once been close, although in the past few years their paths hadn't crossed.

How could Arnie not know him?

The little things began to pile up. Mickey noticed no nods on the street, no smiles from passing strangers. He wanted solitude, so the anonymity was welcome. Still, it seemed odd that three days could pass without an auto-graph seeker or a bashful handshake from a fan.

On the fourth day something bigger happened. Mickey went to an ATM in West Hollywood. He needed some cash so he pulled over at the first one he saw. The machine swallowed his card. Mickey pounded on it. Then he called the number on the screen for people who needed customer service.

A lady answered. Mickey read out his credit card number, which he had memorized.

"I'm sorry, sir. That's not a valid number," she said, kindly enough.

Mickey repeated it slowly. No go. He told her to look in the computer for his name. Nothing there, either. Frustrated, he swore under his breath. His banker would have to straighten this out on Monday. Mickey took out a backup card and inserted it. The machine ate this one, too.

"Sonofabitch."

After that, the weirdness snowballed. He stopped off at a liquor store in Santa Monica to cash a check. The checkout clerk was a bored Arab watching ESPN on an overhead screen. Keeping his eyes glued to the game, he inserted Mickey's check into the cash register, which spit it out.

"No good," the clerk mumbled. He handed the check back.

"There's money in the account. Try it again," said Mickey.

The clerk didn't look at him. "No good. You go away."

Mickey sat in his car in the parking lot of the liquor store. Logic told him that things had moved past the point of coincidence. So what was the message? A flutter of panic rose in his chest, which was natural enough for someone who was on the verge of being erased. Then he remembered something Francisco had told him months ago.

The person you think you are is imaginary. He doesn't exist.

Mickey hadn't reacted when he first heard this. Now he felt himself beginning to shake, and his tremor came from a deep place. He was disappearing. His imagined self was blowing away like scraps of old newspapers in the street. There was no other explanation.

He decided to call Dolores. He waited while the

phone rang, praying that he wouldn't get the machine. What would he say? His mind raced through the possibilities, but there was no time to figure anything out. He would have to play it as it lays.

"Hello?"

"Baby, it's me."

Dolores didn't reply.

On the day that Larry died, Mickey had learned how large the gap could yawn, wide as the Grand Canyon, between what you dread and what you hope for. Now he was experiencing it a second time.

Finally she said, "Who is this?"

Mickey held his breath. There was still a chance.

"It's me, Mickey. You didn't recognize my voice?"

Another pause, but this time he knew there was nothing to hope for. Dolores said, "I don't know who you are, Mickey, but I don't take calls from perverts, and I'm not your baby."

Click.

Mickey felt cold sweat beading on his forehead. He wiped it away with the back of his hand and started the car. He spent the next hour driving around randomly. He could have gone to one of the joints where everybody knew him. He could have leaned out the window of his car and waved at everybody on the sidewalk. But Mickey did none of these things. And the reason was strange.

Why not disappear?

The dread of being erased was evaporating. He wasn't in a screaming panic. Just the opposite. The possibility of shedding the skin he called Mickey Fellows was starting to feel like the right thing, as it might for a snake, or a luna moth emerging from its chrysalis. All at once, Mickey felt incredibly tired of his old self. It was a worn-out husk, nothing more.

Still, he had to make sure.

Alicia answered on the second ring.

"Hi, it's Mickey. We need to talk."

"Hold on. The music's too loud."

Alicia went away to turn it down. For a split second Mickey wondered if this was a last-minute reprieve. Maybe God was saying, "You sure you want to do this?"

Alicia came back on. "If this is about the intellectual property rights, we're not going to get screwed on this deal. Call my attorney."

Mickey took a deep breath. "No, it's me, Mickey. I was working on a new routine. You want to hear the opening?"

"What? Who the hell—"

He hung up before she could finish the sentence. The connection was cut off by a soft click, but it sounded like a loud snap in Mickey's ear, like a rope breaking. He'd gotten enough proof of his nonexistence. Welcome to the unknown. Now he had to figure out how to live with it.

Feelings can't be rushed, so Mickey holed up for a week with the blinds drawn. Not watching TV, not strolling on the beach. He tried taking Payback for a walk one morning, but she growled and he stopped trying to hook her leash. Mickey crouched down beside her.

"Did you hear about the dyslexic who died and went to Hell?" he whispered in her ear. "The guy was in shock. 'This is a mistake,' he cried to the Devil. 'I've been good all my life. What went wrong?' And the Devil says, 'Remember that time you sold your soul to Santa?'"

Payback looked at him dolefully, and put her head down on her paws.

When Mickey found some kids on the beach and gave the dog to them, they were thrilled. Mickey watched her being led away. She didn't look back, and he felt nothing. It was as if he had never owned a dog.

As it turned out, that was the last milestone. Mickey didn't try to sell the house. He had enough cash squirreled away to tide him over until something new happened. He didn't expect to be erased forever.

It might seem, looking from the outside, that Mickey was being punished. He didn't feel that way. The solitary man sitting at the end of Santa Monica pier wasn't lonely. He looked out at the ocean and thought, *I am the ocean*.

He looked up at the sky and thought, *I am the sky*. Wherever he looked he saw himself. It was like being let out of a cage into an eternity that extended in all directions.

This sublime existence was only marred by a tiny scrap of nostalgia. Mickey Fellows had been treated like royalty at the Bel-Air Hotel. He kept being tempted to go back, just to see what that felt like one more time.

One day Mickey gave in. But when he drove up, the valet who took his car gave him a blank look. The doorman glanced at him and went back to whistling for cabs. At the restaurant, the maitre d' looked up, his face expressionless.

Then he smiled. "The gentleman is waiting for you," he murmured.

A waiter in tails led Mickey to a table in the center of the room, where Francisco was sitting.

Mickey didn't know what to say.

"You crossed the line," said Francisco as he sat down.

Without hesitation Mickey said, "Yes, I did. Nobody recognizes me. I broke free."

"Don't abandon this world," said Francisco. "It's the right place to love God. Make the most of it."

Mickey felt amazingly content, and when his order of steamed asparagus with hollandaise arrived, he burst out laughing.

"When I look at this, I *am* asparagus," he said. "It's

ridiculous. I merge with everything. I'm thrilled with everything. I just wonder sometimes if somebody's going to take it all away."

"No, you don't, not really," said Francisco.

There wasn't much else to say during the meal, but toward the end Francisco spoke up. "I came here to see how you were doing. Tell me."

"Everything has become much simpler for me," said Mickey. "I got where you wanted me to go."

"Which was where?" Francisco asked.

"First, beyond fear. When I stopped being afraid, I was safe. Second, beyond ego. When I stopped listening to my ego, I had nothing to prove to anyone. Third, beyond addiction. When I stopped craving the next fix, I was no longer desperate inside."

"So what's next?" asked Francisco.

"I don't know. I'm too new at this," Mickey admitted. "Can you tell me?"

"What is simple now becomes simpler still," said Francisco. "Before, what you experienced was personal happiness. It was based on having a reason to be happy and no reason to be sad. But happiness based on a reason can be snatched away from you at any moment. Now you are happy *without* a reason. That's far more durable. With nothing to like or dislike, you can be happy within yourself. But there is a final stage to be reached, beyond even that."

At this point Francisco stopped explaining. "I want you to know something that is almost impossible to put into words. Do you still have your graduation present?"

Mickey pulled a small velvet bag out of his pocket. He dumped its contents out on the tablecloth: a gold ring, a gold nugget, and a gold signet seal.

Francisco pointed to each. "I told you that this was the secret of happiness. The three objects belonged to a rich collector. When he was asleep, they argued all the time. The gold ring declared it was better than the other two because it was made for the finger of a rich bride. The gold nugget said it was better than the other two because miners had risked their lives to find it. The gold signet said it was better than the other two because it had sealed the messages of a king.

"They argued day and night, until the ring said, 'Let's ask God. He will decide which of us is the best.' The other two agreed, and so they approached the Almighty. Each made its claim for being superior. God listened carefully, and when they were done, he said, 'I can't settle your dispute, I'm sorry.'

"The gold signet seal grew angry. 'What do you mean, you can't settle it? You're God.'

"'That's the problem,' said God. 'I don't see a ring, a nugget, and a seal. All I see is gold.'"

Francisco seemed to be very moved by his little parable. "Do you see?" he asked softly.

"Existence is pure gold. Nothing else is needed," said Mickey. "What will it take for everyone to see that?"

The question hung in the air as they walked outside, then it floated away on the scent of jasmine and plumeria from the hotel's lush garden.

Mickey and Francisco embraced and went their separate ways. Grace, traveling through the universe, had unerringly found its mark. It had sparked one person to new life. That doesn't sound like much, given the billions of people on earth. On the other hand, the ancient sages say—and they must be right—that it takes only one spark to set a whole forest ablaze.

EPILOGUE

SADIE SHUMSKY ALMOST NEVER GOT MAIL. SHE occupied a tiny apartment in assisted living outside Newark, New Jersey, where she grew up. She used to hear from her kid brother Sol, who had left the East a long time ago to make it big in L.A. Then even he quit writing.

"Letter for you," said the charge nurse one day. "Special delivery."

"It must be money," said Sadie, who had practically none.

She almost had a coronary when it actually was money—$175,000. Sol's club in North Hollywood had been sold just before he died. The new owner had sent her, as sole surviving relative, a check for the business. Or rather his lawyers had. The new owner wished to remain anonymous.

Everyone gathered around and cheered. "What will you do with all that money?" they asked. Sadie almost said, "Move out of this dump." But they were good to her here, and if you have to go, it's better to go among friends.

The new owner kept the same staff on when he took over the dive in North Hollywood. He was the solitary type and rarely came in. The bartender and hostess, who amounted to the entire staff, called him "Boss," never by his name, which was a little strange. But he preferred it that way.

You could only be guaranteed to catch the boss on Fridays, which was amateur night. He sat at the back of the room nursing a single Miller Lite all evening. As in the old days, the acts were mostly comics who could only get a gig where there was an open mike.

The audience booed half the acts off the stage before they could finish their set, but the boss always laughed, no matter how awful the gags were. He liked to encourage new talent, and from time to time he had been known to open his own wallet and slip a couple of hundreds to a starving comedian.

Then one night, out of the blue, when the first act was finished, the boss came up to the mike. He tapped it.

"One, two, three, testing."

"What, you have an act?" somebody called out.

"I'm working on some material," the boss said. He cleared his throat. It was a full house, and he had lowered the price of beer. Nobody was feeling any pain.

He picked up the mike and began in a halting voice. "One day a priest, a minister, and a rabbi were out golfing."

The crowd wouldn't let him get to the next line. They let out a collective groan, leading to some serious catcalls.

The boss persisted, leaning closer to the mike. "The rabbi says, 'I bet you a hundred bucks I can make a hole in one.'" He couldn't drown out the crowd, however, and nobody got the punch line once it came. Yet somehow the catcalls didn't seem to faze him.

The boss stood his ground the whole time until he took a bow and stepped off the stage with a smile. It was uncanny to watch him, really. You would have thought, amid all the boos and heckling, that he was listening to someone, somewhere, who was laughing to beat the band.

THE PATH to JOY: TEN PRinCIPLES of SPiriTuaL OPTiMiSM

I S REALITY WHAT WE THINK IT IS? SINCE WE ALL accept the existence of the material world, how could it possibly be the illusion Francisco describes to Mickey in "Why Is God Laughing?" After all, rocks are solid, air sustains life, and the planet revolves on its axis. Yet these facts are not what the word "illusion" refers to. A mystic and a materialist will both stub their toes if they kick a rock. But a mystic believes that the rock is a projection of a deeper reality, while a materialist believes that the rock is all there is—reality doesn't go deeper than things. To a materialist, clouds and mountains are no more than things, their beauty being beside the point. A newborn baby is a thing, too, its humanity being equally beside the point. In a world of things, there is no room for a loving intelligence known as God who presides over creation and gives it meaning.

Yet on the path to joy you discover that meaning is the very basis of life. A baby is a thing only in the most superficial sense. In reality a baby is a field of infinite potential expressing the highest intelligence in Nature. I don't think of this as a mystical belief, but as a truth that lies deeper than the surface picture—where life looks like a stream of random physical events. Meaning is born deep within. Spiritual optimism is also an inner experience. It is based on the love, beauty, creativity, and truth that a person discovers at the level of the soul.

When you explore yourself on the inner plane, you are working with intuition. It's a common misconception that intuition is at odds with science, but Einstein himself said that what separated him from atheists was that "they cannot hear the music of the spheres." In truth, science and spirituality both depend upon intuition, for the greatest scientific discoveries are made through creative leaps, rather than by following a linear trail of established facts.

You use your intuition every day to confirm that you are alive, or that daisies are pretty, or that truth is better than a lie. The path to joy consists of making your intuitions deeper and more accessible. Once my intuition tells me what it is to be alive, then I can explore what my life means, where it came from, and where it's going. Fortunately, there is no force in the universe more powerful than intuition.

On the spiritual path you come to realize certain

basic principles. As these principles unfold, reality shifts. Mere belief cannot transform the events around you, but realization can. It's the difference between believing that you are blessed and actually observing the action of grace in the world.

The principles you will find below are powerful engines for change. As realization grows within you, there is no limit to what you may become; the only certainty is that you will be transformed.

1. THE HEALTHIEST RESPONSE TO LIFE IS LAUGHTER.

This first principle serves as an antidote to fear and sorrow by encouraging you to experience life as joyous. As we begin on the path, joy may come and go in small glimmerings. Yet in the end, laughter will dispel suffering like so much smoke and dust. Suffering is one of illusion's most convincing aspects, but it is still unreal.

A golden rule applies here: *What is true in the material world is false in God's world, and vice versa.* In this case, the material world seems to be dominated by crisis and suffering, and therefore the sanest way to approach life is with worry, anxiety, and defensiveness. But once your consciousness shifts, you realize that life itself couldn't exist without an underlying creativity, and that this continuous act of creation is in itself an expression of ecstasy. These qualities are the basis of your life, also.

In fact, the lens of materialism gives us the least accurate view of the world, because through it we see consciousness as merely an accidental by-product of brain chemistry, and the powers of the mind as a myth. To equate the deepest reality with inert atoms colliding with each other in the dead cold of outer space denies all that sustains life and makes it worth living: beauty, truth, art, love, morality, community, discovery, curiosity, inner growth, and higher consciousness.

What do all these qualities have in common? They depend on intuition. There is no objective proof that love is beautiful, or that the truth can set you free. Rather, you must come to these realizations through your own inner experience. On the spiritual path everything depends on a shift in consciousness; nothing depends on atoms colliding.

What we have, then, is two opposing worldviews contending for your allegiance. Is it better to be spiritual or materialistic? Is God a mere add-on to physical existence, or at the very root of existence? This isn't an easy choice to make, because the evidence is seriously out of balance. Most of us have extensive personal knowledge of the material world, but scant personal knowledge of

God. God has a lot of proving to do. He must prove that he's present and dependable, the same way a rock or a tree is. If we want to claim that God sustains life, he must sustain it as viably as air, water, and food do. In other words, to realize God is no small thing. It may take a lifetime—if you're lucky.

To begin this journey, commit yourself to the possibility that everything you see around you is far less real than God. You want to see the truth "with all your heart, with all your soul, and with all your mind," as Jesus says. This is actually a commitment to joy. When you feel momentary happiness, or you want to burst out laughing, or you smile for no apparent reason, you are glimpsing eternal reality. For a fleeting moment the curtain has parted so you can experience something beyond the illusion. In time these moments of joy will begin to knit together. Instead of the exception, they will become the norm. There is no better way to know that you are growing in God-realization.

2. THERE IS ALWAYS A REASON TO BE GRATEFUL.

This second principle is an antidote to victimization. It establishes that you are seen and provided for. The more you notice the truth of this principle, the less you will believe that you are a victim.

Looking around, it's obvious that life is orderly. A bee flies from flower to flower, eating and pollinating in accordance with a magnificent, ordered scheme. Millions of years of evolution have exquisitely matched bee and flower so that neither can exist without the other. Why, then, do we believe that our own lives can't be effortlessly sustained? One major obstacle is that we see ourselves as victims. Our bodies are subject to aging and death. Accidents are unavoidable. Catastrophe and disaster looms just around the corner, controlled by a whimsical destiny. And simply imagining the terrible things that can happen to you brings as much suffering as the events themselves.

Being a victim is the logical result of being in constant danger. If God sustains us, then surely he must reverse this whole scheme of random accidents that puts everyone in peril. This is a tricky point, however, because we are also surrounded by abundance in Nature. Optimists point to our green earth overflowing with life, nourishment, and beauty. However, can a loving God really supply us with life's good things one day and pain the next? Most people who feel grateful to God tend to deny that he is also responsible for disease, calamity, and death. Yet an all-knowing, all-powerful deity can't be responsible for only part of what goes on. Either he sustains everything or nothing.

The way to escape from living under a God who brings pleasure one day and pain the next is to realize that God isn't a person. We only call God "he" because our minds resist thinking of God as a total abstraction. In truth, being total, God has to be abstract. You can't wrap your mind around the All. Instead, we wrap our minds around the things we notice, and choose to believe in.

To the extent that you notice God in your life, acknowledge him with gratitude. God doesn't need to be thanked—after all, he already has everything, including thanks. But by choosing gratitude you are selecting a benevolent aspect of the All on which you want to focus.

The purpose of gratitude is to connect yourself to a higher vision of life. You have the power to choose whether to activate the aspect of God that gives or the aspect that takes away. Whatever you pay attention to will grow. If you pay attention to those aspects of God that demonstrate love, truth, beauty, intelligence, order, and spiritual evolution, those aspects will begin to expand in your life. Bit by bit, like a mosaic, disparate fragments of grace will merge to form a complete picture. Eventually this picture will replace the more threatening one you have carried around inside you since infancy.

The external world claims to be real, but it, too, is an image created in consciousness and projected outward. Once you realize that you alone are the projector of reality, you will no longer be dominated by external events. You will correct the mistake that lies at the very root of victimization: a belief that the movie controls you, instead of the other way around.

3. YOU BELONG IN THE SCHEME OF THE UNIVERSE. THERE'S NOTHING TO BE AFRAID OF. YOU ARE SAFE.

The third principle is the antidote for insecurity. It tells us that fear can be totally convincing, yet there is no truth to it. Fear cannot be trusted.

In modern life we are taught to respect fear as an essential contributor to our survival, a biological signal that alerts mind and body to approaching danger. But the ancient sages of India taught that fear was born of duality; when human beings realized that they were no longer part of God, they immediately became afraid of what might happen to them. In the twentieth century, after two devastating world wars and the advent of the atomic bomb, this haunting insecurity was promoted into an inescapable fact of life, which came to be known as existential anxiety. You and I are children of an era when simply to be alive seemed to be taking the ultimate risk. As a result, we fall prey to anxiety about who we are and where we belong.

On the spiritual path you can completely recover from such anxiety. By rejecting fear a little at a time, you come to realize that life isn't constantly at risk. You are safe, you are seen, and you are cared for. Moving from fear to fearlessness requires a shift in orientation because we live in a climate of fear, where it's all too easy to succumb to a constant barrage of potential threats. The morning news pulls us into a dark world of constant disasters, which is reinforced by the evening news. To counter this, you must look to your own inner guidance. Realize that what makes you safe is a higher intelligence that resides within you. Potential dangers are illusions. Only what lies at hand is real.

I'm not saying that existence can be sanitized of all its discomforts and sudden reversals of fortune. I'm offering the possibility of approaching existence from a different perspective. You will be secure once you realize that God has provided you with everything you need to meet the challenges of life, whatever they may be. You are standing center stage in your own personal drama. Surrounding you is a much larger stage, and if you find yourself in dangerous times on that larger stage, danger will be present. However, this situation is very different from seeing yourself living inside a swirling chaos of impending doom. The point is to take your place inside the drama with confidence. Everything is as it should be.

The role assigned to you is right and proper. It is tailor-made for you, for your complete self. And your complete self won't settle for a listless, uneventful existence. The fact that life isn't completely risk free doesn't change the fact that it's driven by choices made at the soul level. The voice of fear tries to convince you that you are a helpless victim of chance. The very opposite is true. At the deepest level, the level of the soul, you are the author of everything that happens to you.

4. YOUR SOUL CHERISHES EVERY ASPECT OF YOUR LIFE.

The fourth principle is the antidote for feeling undervalued. It states that your worth is absolute, and that everything that happens to you—whether it feels good at the time or not—is part of a divine plan unfolding from the level of the soul.

As we've seen, the values that drive the material world must be reversed entirely if you want to realize God. In the conventional view, self-worth comes down to having a strong ego. People who possess strong egos feel self-confident. They enjoy asserting themselves against obstacles. They meet challenges, and in return life gives them money, status, and possessions—external rewards for external accomplishment.

In that light, it's almost embarrassing that Jesus teaches exactly the opposite—to be loved by God, one must be innocent, humble, a servant to all men. But Jesus' view accords with the great wisdom traditions, which hold that a person's worth doesn't change depending on external success and its rewards. A person's worth is the value of a soul, which is infinite. Since every event in your life isn't happening just to a person but to a soul, everything in life should be cherished.

We all know that life has its ups and downs, and that our sense of self-worth rises and falls accordingly. Napoleon was a titan when he won victories on the battlefield but a dwarf after Waterloo. In a world of change, we ego-driven people seem to be puppets to every whim of circumstance. Yet from the soul's point of view, change occurs against the backdrop of nonchange; the basis of existence is eternal, unmoved, steady, and all encompassing.

How can you shift your attention away from change? I am largely unconvinced by people who say that they feel the real, immediate presence of God, Jesus, or their souls. Those are extremely advanced attainments on the spiritual path, certainly not among the first doors that open on the journey. But I do know that I can experience myself, so now my job is to find the part of myself that doesn't change. Clearly my mind changes all the time, as quickly as the next thought, and so does my body, as quickly as the next skin cell sloughing off or the next heartbeat. So the search for nonchange must take me elsewhere.

This is where meditation proves most useful. When you meditate, you shift your focus. Instead of paying attention to the surface of the mind, which teems with constant change, you go deeper to experience silence. In and of itself, silence is pointless. Life is about action and response, not silent detachment. But inner silence is something far more profound: it is awareness being aware of itself, also known as wakefulness, or mindfulness.

In its silent depths, your mind knows everything that's going on. Time collapses into a single focal point, where the one unshakable thing you know is "I am." This isn't passive knowledge. It is the center of everything, the source of all the activity that springs forth as thoughts, sensations, and external events. Silence, it turns out, is the womb of creation. Therefore, meditation is a creative event through which you are reclaiming authorship of your life.

Now we see what meditating twenty-four hours a day actually means: you retain your alertness and wakefulness all the time. Once you have authorship of your self, you come out of silence into activity to write your own story. Now there is no difference between sitting in meditation and living in the world. Both are expressions of awareness, the one silent, and the other active. Now you maintain two types of attention, one devoted to change, the other to nonchange. This is the shift in consciousness that allows you to live from the level of the soul.

5. THERE IS A PLAN, AND YOUR SOUL KNOWS WHAT IT IS.

The fifth principle is the antidote to meaninglessness. It states that your life has a purpose. You determine that purpose at the soul level, and then that purpose unfolds in daily life as part of the divine plan. The more deeply you are connected to the plan, the more powerful it becomes in your life. Ultimately nothing can stop it.

When writing about the spiritual path, I reach a point where I wish I could dispense with terminology like soul, God, and spirit. Because there is only one reality, we don't need a separate, mundane vocabulary for everyday existence, and another, special vocabulary for higher existence. Either everything is spiritual or nothing is. In God's eyes, walking on water is no more miraculous than the ability of hemoglobin to bond with oxygen inside a red blood corpuscle. Neither is readily visible, and both belong to the infinitely unfolding scheme of creation.

Yet it would seem that a life full of purpose and meaning must be closer to God than a life spent in aimless confusion. Dualism has a powerful hold on the mind, so we can't help but think in terms of high and low, better and worse. What's hard to comprehend is that God, wanting nothing, also demands nothing of us. In spiritual terms, no life is more or less worthy. Today's thief will be reborn as tomorrow's saint, and vice versa.

In a divine plan everyone has a part. And because God is within you, you yourself have an absolute right to choose your part in the divine plan. How does that plan work in practical terms? A central feature is the issue of perception.

When you were a baby, you perceived yourself in a very limited way. What you couldn't handle or understand was given over to your father and mother. They fed you until you could feed yourself, provided shelter until you could provide it for yourself, and so on. As you became more capable, your sense of where you stood in relation to the world changed. In other words, with each step toward self-sufficiency, your perception shifted.

The divine plan is like that. At first, personal power is very limited. The ego assumes it must provide for itself by grabbing what it wants and rejecting the rest. Perception at this stage is limited to the individual; the scope for vision is quite narrow. What benefits "I, me, and mine" is all that matters. The ego has no regard for how the self is interconnected with everything else. Ironically, it's at this stage, when we've given external forces the authority to dictate events, that the ego feels most powerful.

As perception expands, so does inner potential. Beyond the ego a wider circle that includes "I, me, and mine" expands in all directions. In the divine plan, a person can expand without limit on the level of the soul. You begin to witness how incredibly creation has been organized, with what perfect care and infinite intelligence. Since God has infinite intelligence, the more your perception expands, the closer you come to God. There's not even a need to seek, only to see.

In the end, everything is already God, so it's just a matter of seeing more and more deeply until God is revealed. You acquire a vision that is attuned to the finest aspects of beauty and truth. One of the great blessings of existence is that everyone is born with a desire to see more. That's why the sages of India believed that even to think about God is a sign that surely he will one day appear. It turns out that expansion of consciousness *is* the divine plan. There is no other. As your awareness keeps growing, you become more and more certain that you are part of the divine plan as well. Nothing more is demanded of you, or ever was.

6. ECSTASY IS THE ENERGY OF SPIRIT. WHEN LIFE FLOWS, ECSTASY IS NATURAL.

The sixth principle is the antidote to inertia. It states that infinite energy is available to you. You are a co-creator with God. To claim your creative power, you need only connect with the primal energies at play within you.

How do you know if you are connected to God? One of the simplest indications is the way your life flows. If you feel stuck, if inertia and habit rule your day, then your connection to God is tenuous. On the other hand, if you are certain that what you want in life is unfolding day by day, your connection with God is strong. Creative flow is the operating rule of the cosmos.

Just as creation takes myriad forms, so does energy. On the spiritual path you discover many types of energy.

Mostly we rely on superficial energies generated by the ego: anger, fear, competitive drive, the desire to achieve, and love that makes us feel desirable. There is no right or wrong in the domain of energy, but the ego falls prey to the illusion that *only* anger, fear, the drive to achieve, and so on, are real. It ignores higher energies and lower ones, which is why the ego becomes so isolated.

Lower energies dominate the body and its intricate operations. "Lower" is a misleading term, since the body's intelligence is just as great as any in creation, but for all its astonishing organizing power, the body is satisfied to be guided by the mind. The body's intelligence is humble, with no need to dominate or achieve; for the body, fitting perfectly into the natural order is joy enough. The ego could learn a lot from the body, but it rarely does.

At the same time, the ego also shuts out higher energies. These are the subtle forces of the soul: love, compassion, truth, and the knowledge of God. The soul has no reason to compete with ego because the soul has already attained the highest position in creation—unity with God. Like circles of angels in medieval Christian paintings, revolving around the heavenly throne singing God's praises, the soul is content to experience its own ecstasy and to celebrate it without end. The ego believes, wrongly, that such bliss is either a fiction or can only be attained

through externals—more sex, money, status, and possessions.

Finally, there is the subtlest energy of all, the original
stuff from which everything else is made. This energy lies
on the fine line between existence and nonexistence. It's
the first quiver of the creative impulse, the first wisp of
God's thought. In most spiritual traditions this vibration
is known as "I am." Nothing could exist without it, yet
nothing is more delicate. When experienced personally,
it feels like pure ecstasy, or bliss-consciousness.

The full range of these energies powers your life, and
all of them are available to you. The kind of energy you
can call upon at any given moment, however, depends on
your level of consciousness. At a gross level, if someone
wants an apple, she must work to get the money to buy
one. At a more subtle level, if she wants an apple, someone happens to walk in the room with an apple in hand.
At the very subtlest level, if she wants an apple, an apple
appears. The ego—and the world at large—only believes
in the gross level of energy. But all of us experience subtle
energies from time to time: wishes come true, desires
manifest, and invisible forces seem to be at play.

On the spiritual path a person proceeds into subtler
and subtler realms of the mind, and with each step new
levels of energy become available. Finally, when unity
with God is attained, all energy becomes available. At

that point, your wishes and desires are the same as God's. You have always been a potential co-creator, and when you realize God, that potential is fully activated. Everything you imagine comes into being spontaneously, as easily as the thought itself. There could be no other way, since in unity a thought and a thing are one and the same.

7. THERE IS A CREATIVE SOLUTION TO EVERY PROBLEM. EVERY POSSIBILITY HOLDS THE PROMISE OF ABUNDANCE.

The seventh principle is the antidote to failure. It tells us that every question includes its own answer. The only reason a problem arises before its solution is that our minds are limited—we think in terms of sequences, of before and after. Outside the narrow boundaries of time, problems and solutions arise at the same instant.

Modern society is oriented toward solving problems. There is no lack of go-getters who dedicate themselves to finding new ways to do things, and no shortage of belief that progress can't be stopped. Much of this confidence, however, is a distraction. By focusing on the next technology, the next engineering marvel, the next medical breakthrough, we lose sight of deeper problems that offer no solution. Buddha pointed to the problem of suffering, Jesus to the problem of sin and the lack of love, Gandhi to the absence of peace in a world of violence. What new technology will prevent me from attacking my enemy? What medical breakthrough will enable me to love my neighbor as myself?

You can look around and see how futile external solutions have proven. Crime, famine, war, epidemics, and poverty continue to baffle us, and yet society throws money at these problem over and over, as if a failed approach will succeed if only we persist. On the spiritual path you discover that all problems are rooted in consciousness, therefore the solution is always a shift in consciousness.

If you were to be happy from the soul level, totally in accord with God, what would that be like? In a word, it would be effortless. To be happy from the soul level, three things are required:

> You act without effort.
> You feel joy in what you do.
> Your actions bring results.

All three requirements must work together if you want to experience the happiness God intended. It is already on display in the natural kingdom, where every creature acts spontaneously, and yet every action supports the entire ecological system. Human beings, however, primarily reside in a mental landscape. Our vision of ourselves rules what we do; the physical environment comes second (if at all), and it is expected to adapt to our demands.

In Nature, every challenge is met with a response. As dinosaurs die out, mammals thrive. As ferns give way to flowering plants, insects learn to feed on pollen. Creation and destruction move together, constantly in touch with each other. The same seamless interaction is also possible in a mental ecological system. In higher states of consciousness, no gap appears between desire and fulfillment. Few of us experience this spontaneous state, however. The conventional condition of separation is all about gaps and discontinuity. Desires seem to lead to failure. The best-laid plans seem to go astray, and our experience of separation seems to grow.

You might think it would take heroic efforts to solve the problems that face us. Spiritually speaking, the reverse is true. The soul's vision isn't about struggle and lack of results. It isn't about failure. You only need to measure your actions against the three simple conditions I mentioned above.

Am I acting easily, without struggle?
Do I enjoy what I'm doing?
Are results coming of their own accord?

Answering "yes" means that spiritually you are going in the right direction; answering "no" means that you aren't.

I have a friend who has spent years giving money and advice to his family. Of four brothers, he is the only one who went to college and became a successful doctor. He's confident and quick to offer solutions, and for years he thought he knew what his less fortunate brothers should be doing with their lives.

Recently a crisis arose. The brothers, never very good at finding work, began to fall into debt. They wanted more and more money from my friend, and when he threatened to cut them off, they became angry.

"Look at this," he said in disgust, holding up an e-mail from his youngest brother. "He says that if I don't give him more money, I'm guilty of abuse."

I asked him how much gratitude his brothers had expressed over the years.

My friend shook his head. "They've taken my money and totally ignored me."

"And yet you continue with the same program," I pointed out.

"I have to. I can't bear the idea of having my brothers wind up on welfare or going to jail after doing something desperate," he said.

At this point I raised the three criteria for action. "Is it easy to help your brothers?" I asked. No, he admitted, they resisted every step of the way.

"Are you happy dealing with them?" I asked. No, he said. He was frustrated and miserable. He'd often considered changing his phone number so that he'd never have to talk to them again.

Finally I asked, "Are you getting results?" Clearly he wasn't. Instead of improving their lives, my friend's money and advice only enabled them to stay stuck in their old ways.

When no amount of thinking, scheming, struggle, persuasion, and force will alter a situation, it's time to apply the three simple questions I posed to my friend. All you and I can do is to take on our own role in the divine scheme. Infinite intelligence provides solutions to every problem. In the case of plants and animals, ecology balances itself; the individual plant and animal only has to play its part. Human beings are more ambitious—we want to create our own visions and carry them out, which makes things more complicated. But the same basic laws apply.

This seems like a good place to bring up one of the

persistent charges leveled against people on the spiritual path: they are selfish and self-indulgent; in a world suffocating with problems, spiritual seekers only think about their own well-being, using God as a convenient cover. Essentially, what this criticism comes down to is a claim that the ego dictates what so-called spiritual people do, just as it does for everyone. That can be a legitimate point. If you see yourself on the path to God because he's the biggest prize of all, the ultimate lottery win, then certainly ego is in charge.

Yet when the spiritual path takes us beyond the worship of "I, me, and mine," the expansion of consciousness melts the boundaries of separation. You begin to see yourself not in isolation but as part of the whole. It becomes possible to help others as you would help yourself, not because service and charity make you feel good, but because you recognize that you are the very person you serve. The ego is capable of offering service to the poor and suffering, but when it does, there's an ulterior motive: giving to others makes the ego feel superior.

I know countless sincere seekers, however, who measure their rewards in terms of peace, compassion, and intimacy with their souls. Spiritual growth doesn't require a life of service. Such a life can be as miserable and selfish as any other. But I would venture that spiritual seekers do more to alleviate human suffering than any government. Every step toward God-realization benefits humanity as a whole.

8. OBSTACLES ARE OPPORTUNITIES IN DISGUISE.

The eighth principle is the antidote to inflexibility. It tells us that obstacles are signals from consciousness that we need to change direction, to take a new tack. If your mind is open, it will perceive the next opportunity to do so.

When the ego encounters an obstacle, it responds by exerting more force. The ego's world is a battlefield where you have to fight to win. There's no doubt that this attitude can bring results—every empire was built by force of conquest—but it does so at a terrible cost: the tide of war, struggle, and destruction continues to rise. When you are attacked there is a great temptation to adopt the weapons of ego in retaliation. How many peace movements are full of angry activists? How many environmentalists love the earth but hate those who despoil it? As Mother Teresa famously said, she wasn't willing to join an antiwar movement because it wasn't the same as a peace movement.

The ego's world presents a massive obstacle to spiritual growth. Therefore, the need to be flexible arises every day. You will meet with inner resistance as a constant occurrence, with intermittent victories and moments of joy. To avoid discouragement, you need to realize that obstacles come from the same source as everything else. God isn't only present in the good moments. An infinite intelligence has found a way to fit every hour of your life into a plan. From day to day you can't possibly comprehend the incredibly intricate connections between your life and the cosmos. The entire universe had to conspire to bring about this very moment in time.

You can't plan in advance how to meet the next challenge, yet most people try to do just that. They protect themselves against worst-case scenarios; they cling to a small repertoire of habits and reactions; they narrow their lives to family, friends, and work. Husbanding your resources may bring a modicum of security, but by doing so you will have completely shut out the unknown, which is the same as hiding your potential from yourself. How will you know what you are capable of if you don't open yourself to life's mysteries, or usher in the new? For life to remain fresh at every moment, your response must break free from your established patterns.

The secret is to abandon old habits and trust in spontaneity. By definition, being spontaneous cannot be planned in advance. It doesn't have to be. Whenever you catch yourself reacting in an old, familiar way, simply stop. Don't invent a new reaction; don't fall back on the opposite of what you usually do. Instead, ask for openness. Go inside, be with yourself, and allow the next reaction to come of its own accord.

A famous Broadway composer once was asked how he came up with his wonderful tunes. He had been known to pull his car off the side of the road in the middle of busy traffic to write down a hit song. What was his secret? "Wait, drift, and obey," he said.

Exactly.

9. EVOLUTION LEADS THE WAY THROUGH DESIRE.

The ninth principle is the antidote to hypocrisy. It encourages us to act on our genuine desires, because they show the way to real growth. Don't pretend to be better—or other—than you are. Don't fall into the trap of having one face for the world and another for God. Who you really are is exactly who you should be.

Desire has become a huge problem for modern people. Two forces pull us in opposite directions. One liberates us from old values. The other wants to preserve those values. The resulting polarization can be seen in every sphere of life, especially the social and political realms. Churchgoers feel righteous, responsible, and obedient to God's will. They view anyone unlike themselves as devoid of values, and therefore unworthy of God's love. By denying God to all those who have strayed from the path of righteousness, the devout are unwittingly taking on themselves a role that belongs only to God.

This schism can also be seen in our inner conflicts. At bottom, the pull of old values is restrictive. Its God is judgmental, and his demands are not to be flouted. In other words, spirit exists to rebuke the flesh and keep its appetites under control. The force of liberation, on the other hand, evokes a God of tolerance who loves his creation and asks only for love in return. To heal this schism, we need to realize that God makes no demands and sets no particular limits of any kind, on thought, word, or deed.

At the beginning of the path, it doesn't matter whether you are devout or atheist. What both sides have in common is constraint. The prevailing condition has a narrow vision—we all share it. So, how does God want us to grow, in what direction, according to what guidelines? None. You get to grow the way you want to, by following your own desires. You are already growing the right seeds. The things that deeply interest you play the role of God; you feel an irresistible attraction to them.

The visible world in all its details is a symbol for God. You can gaze at the sky on a warm June day, stay glued to TV looking at football, or watch your infant child asleep in the cradle. Whatever captivates you is also trying to wake you up. A friend of mine put it more bluntly: "If you don't know where you're going, it doesn't matter where you start." An impulse of love, if followed wherever it leads, will become richer and more intense, and in the end it will reveal itself as divine. An impulse of gratitude will do the same thing, as will compassion, kindness, charity, faith, devotion, appreciation, art, and science. Wherever the human mind wants to expand, God will be waiting at the end of the line.

10. FREEDOM IS LETTING GO.

The tenth principle is the antidote to attachment. It reminds us that striving isn't the way to God. If you let go of what isn't real in your life, what's left will be real: what's left is God alone.

Over the years I've found that letting go baffles people. They are eager to let go of things that bring pain and suffering, yet by some perverse irony, the shackles refuse to drop away. Abused spouses don't walk out on their abusers. Addicts reach for more of what is destroying them. Anger, fear, and violence roam the mind at will, even though a person has tried with all his might to renounce them. How do you let go of stuff that is attached to you so stubbornly?

Telling someone who's stuck to "just let go" is as futile as telling someone who is hysterical to "just calm down." Negative things stick to us because they are tied to an underlying energy that doesn't want to move away. Angry people don't need a specific reason to get angry; they only need a pretext for releasing the pent-up energy that keeps them at a constant simmer. Anxious people are worried inside, not about any one thing, but about fear itself. To be free, you must find a way to let go of all the stuck energy that keeps sending out the same old messages. The ability to let go is more complex than it sounds, but nothing is more crucial.

Let's look more closely at anger and fear, the two emotional energies that most persistently haunt us. Letting go of anger and fear requires a process, which includes the following:

Be alert. Don't ignore your feelings when you are angry or anxious. Resist the impulse to look away and shove your feelings back down out of sight. The more alert you are, the easier it will be to access stuck energy and let it go.

Be objective. If you identify personally with negativity, you will never let it go. Learn to see anger as only energy, like electricity. Electricity isn't about you. Neither is anger. It's universal and sticks to anything that seems unfair or unjust. Fear sticks to anything that feels dangerous or unsafe.

Detach from the specifics. Energies get stuck to particular situations: a specific person rams your car from the rear, butts in line ahead of you at the supermarket, or cheats you out of money. These are the contents of the situation, its specifics, and you cannot completely let go of energy by living solely in those moments. Imagine having a fight with your spouse. You are sure you're justified in your position. But if you refuse to stop being angry until your spouse says, "I was wrong; you were right all along," you could wait forever. And even if he does apologize, your anger might not completely disappear. Detach from the contents of the situation and release your anger by yourself, for your own good.

Take responsibility. This goes hand in hand with detachment. Your energy is yours and nobody else's. In spiritual terms, it doesn't matter who is right or wrong, who is the aggressor or the victim. The only important thing is how to win your own freedom. In a world of opposites, right and wrong are engaged in an eternal struggle. Your role is to let go of energy that has stuck to you for whatever reason. Once you take responsibility, you won't be tossed about at the whim of circumstance.

Don't expect anyone to do it for you. There is certainly such a thing as divine guidance, but the road to freedom is through the self. Most of us hope to gain strength from other people, not some divine agency. Yet there is no getting around the fact that all you have for the spiritual journey is your own mind, body, and soul. As much as others can offer solace and helpful wishes, only you can embark on the journey inside yourself.

Let your body participate. Letting go isn't just a mental process. In fact, you have metabolized your past and given it sanctuary in your body. Or as someone put it simply, "The issues are in the tissues." Many kinds of bodywork and purification therapies can be useful here. To begin with, let your body do what it wants to do. It knows how to tremble with fear and convulse with anger. Don't resist the body's natural reactions, but don't inflict them on someone else, either. Throwing off stuck energy is a private process that belongs to you alone.

Explore and discover. I don't want to imply that the spiritual journey involves laborious effort undertaken in solitude. Quite the contrary. Nothing is more fascinating than finding out who you really are, and what you are really about. The vast majority of people live secondhand lives. All they know about themselves is what others tell them; the voices they hear in their heads come from the past; their vision of possibilities amounts to what they were taught at school, in church, and in the family. The past creates unresolved energy. The need to conform creates a fear of breaking free. Fortunately, to the extent that you let go of these old energies, you will win a new bit of freedom.

Value freedom above everything. I said earlier that we all hear two impulses inside ourselves. One says, "This is what I want to do," the other says, "This is what I'd better do." The first is the voice of freedom; the second is the voice of fear. The divine plan is infinitely complex, but when it comes down to each person, it's infinitely simple. You get to be whoever you want to be; you get to do whatever you want to do. That's not the same as what your ego wants you to be or what your fantasies urge you to do. Spiritual freedom releases you into infinite Being. Then and only then will you encounter the real you. At that moment, all that you wanted to be in the past will be seen as a temporary impulse. And each impulse to be free will been seen to be leading you in the right direction.

YOUR STUCK ENERGIES force you to be someone who doesn't exist anymore: the angry child deprived of love, the frightened child who doesn't feel safe. The past is a false guide to the future, and yet it's what most of us rely upon. By letting go of stuck energies, you let go of your past. Go deep enough and you can let go of time itself. In that release lies ultimate freedom. All of human history rests in you. Yours is the grief of the world and its sorrows, and its fear and anger. Some might feel despair to hear this truth, but why not feel joy? To think that in liberating yourself you liberate the world. What stakes could be higher?

I once read that Jesus, Buddha, and all the saints and sages exist for but one reason: "to precipitate reality upon the earth." In that moment I saw humanity as a giant pyramid, with each person perched in his or her own unique spot. God descends to earth like fresh spring rain, and at every level his grace is received differently. For some it feels like love, for others like salvation. It feels like safety and warmth at one level, like coming home at another. I'm not sure where I belong in the pyramid, because I have chosen to be a climber. I push myself to keep moving up, inspired by occasional glimpses of the level of consciousness I must attain.

One day I will reach the very pinnacle. At that rarefied height I doubt that I will see an image of Buddha or Christ, or whoever has been blessed to come before me. They will have vanished into the ether. Above me will be only the vast expanse of All, the infinite blissful plenitude of God. But my impulse won't be to look upward, but not because I am afraid to see the divine face to face. I want to look down instead, because you will be coming toward me, barely a few steps back. We will see each other at last in the light of God, and in that moment of recognition what I can only describe as love will arise like a never-ending dawn.

ACKNOWLEDGMENTS

To my editor, Peter Guzzardi, for skillfully winnowing out my verbosity; to Carolyn Rangel and my staff at the Chopra Center, whose dedication inspires me every single day; to my family at home, and my family at Harmony Books: Thank you, Shaye, Jenny, Julia, Kira, and Tara.

About the Author

DEEPAK CHOPRA is the author of more than fifty books translated in over thirty-five languages, including numerous *New York Times* bestsellers in both the fiction and nonfiction categories. He is also founder and president of the Alliance for a New Humanity. *Time* magazine heralds Deepak Chopra as one of the top one hundred heroes and icons of the century, and credits him as "the poet-prophet of alternative medicine."

Visit the author at DeepakChopra.com